SIMPLY SOFT FOOD

200 delicious and nutritious recipes
for people with chewing difficulty
or who simply enjoy soft food

Kristine K. Benishek, MLS, AHIP

Simply Soft Food: 200 delicious and nutritious recipes for people with chewing difficulty or who simply enjoy soft food

ENDORSEMENTS

"This cookbook fills an important need. The population in the United States is aging, and many older adults will be faced with the need to maintain proper nutrition while their ability to effectively chew food is reduced. Developed over the years through trial and error, this book will be a very valuable aid for older adults and those who care for them."
Ira B. Lamster, D.D.S., M.M.Sc., Dean Emeritus
Columbia University College of Dental Medicine
Editor of *Improving Oral Health for the Elderly: An Interdisciplinary Approach*
New York City, NY

"This is an absolutely delicious book! Every recipe can be enjoyed by those who have to eat soft foods as well as the general population. Ms. Benishek's insightful book has taken us into the 21st century where those who still enjoy eating but require soft food now have an excellent cookbook to rely on. Bravo!"
Sharon Otto Trekell, PhD
Director, Inner Well Institute
Certified Health and Wellness Coach
Dayton, OH

"This is a great resource for anyone faced with preparing satisfying and nutritious soft-food meals over an extended period without multiple re-runs. Her approach and commentary is warm and down-to-earth. Simply Soft Food is a real gift for those with chewing problems who want to maintain an optimal quality of life."
Suzanne Hughes, MSN, RN
Director of Population Health, Summa Health System
Associate Editor of *CardioSource*
Akron, OH

ACKNOWLEDGMENT

The idea for this cookbook came when my aging parents, Jerome and Marjorie Benishek, began asking me to cook soft foods as it had become difficult for them to eat hard, crunchy or chewy foods. I thank them for taste-testing every one of these recipes to make sure the recipes are soft enough and tasty enough to be included. I also thank my brothers David, Gary and Terry, sister-in-law Betty, plus the many nieces, nephews, and friends who taste-tested the recipes, giving their honest comments on recipes to ensure all recipes in this book are worthy of including. I also thank my friend Lorraine Bachand for giving her support and professional advice during the writing of this book. Many thanks go to the healthcare professionals who saw value in having this cookbook of soft food recipes available to their patients and to the community. I appreciate their generosity in offering to endorse this book: Ira B. Lamster, D.D.S., M.M.Sc., Dean, Columbia University College of Dental Medicine; Suzanne Hughes, MSN, RN, Director of Population Health, Summa Health System; and Sharon Otto Trekell, PhD, Director, Inner Well Institute.

CONTENTS

INTRODUCTION

Simply Soft Food is written for the millions of otherwise healthy people who cannot eat hard, crunchy, or chewy foods due to a wide variety of reasons, such as the elderly who have lost some teeth or have lost chewing strength, people who wear dentures or orthodontic braces, those who have temporomandibular joint disorders, and a wide variety of other reasons that may prevent someone from eating hard to chew foods. This cookbook will allow everyone who is restricted to a diet of tender and easy to chew foods to fully enjoy a wide variety of delicious, satisfying foods without feeling limited by what they can eat.

The idea for this book began when my elderly parents started to say "we can only eat soft food now". I found myself racking my brain for recipes. What to cook? Our family staples had always been things like steaks, roasts, pork chops - in short, anything we could sink our teeth into! While there are many soft food recipes "out there", when suddenly faced with having to cook only soft foods, it is difficult to remember them all. As one of 76 million Baby Boomers, it occurred to me that if I was having the problem of needing to cook only soft foods for elderly parents, there were a lot of other people in the same situation. Later, when I developed temporomandibular joint problems after an injury, I realized that there are many people who need to eat soft foods for a wide variety of reasons. So, I figured that if I was going to spend the time coming up with soft recipes that my parents and I could eat and enjoy, why not share them? *Simply Soft Food* pulls together many traditional favorites, plus a few not-so-traditional ones, into one book so people won't need to rack their brains with "what can I make?"

This cookbook has over 200 recipes of tasty and satisfying soft foods, including 60 main dishes, 20 soft sandwiches, over 20 breakfast "anytime" dishes, 40 side dishes, as well as delicious bread, soup, and dessert recipes. Main dishes are arranged by the most used home-cooking styles: stovetop cooking, oven dishes, and slow cooker meals. This was done to accommodate a cook's often varying schedule. Sometimes a person wants to quickly throw something into the slow cooker in the morning before dashing out the door to spend a long day elsewhere while at other times a hectic day means a person only has time to grab the frying pan to cook something quickly. Each recipe has step-by-step directions that can be easily followed.

My intention in writing this book is to assist others who are in the situation of needing to find a variety of soft food recipes and wanting the foods to be both satisfying and nutritious. Because people who are limited by what they can eat often do not get enough nutrients, they are at a very real risk of malnutrition. For this reason, each recipe is written with nutrition in mind, and even the desserts have a nutritional component.

While there are millions of people who need soft foods for a variety of reasons there are few resources to help them find recipes that will allow them to fully enjoy a wide variety of delicious, satisfying foods without feeling limited by what they can eat. These are wonderful, home-cooking style recipes that can be enjoyed by all, regardless of age or whether or not they have chewing problems. Good food is a fundamental pleasure in life. This cookbook will take away the pressure of finding enough soft food recipes to allow variety, giving everyone the pleasure of a good meal.

BREADS

APPLE PEAR COFFEE CAKE

I made this coffee cake for the first time many years ago, and it continues to be a huge success every time I make it. You can't go wrong with this tasty treat. The batter is fairly stiff, but after folding in the fruit it bakes into a light, moist coffee cake.

2 cups all-purpose or light baking flour
1½ teaspoons baking powder
¾ teaspoon baking soda
¼ teaspoon salt
½ cup butter, softened
¾ cup sugar
2 eggs
1 teaspoon vanilla
1 cup sour cream
1¼ cups cooking apples, peeled, finely chopped or
  shredded
1 pear, peeled, finely chopped
3 tablespoons cinnamon sugar

Heat oven to 350 degrees

1. In a medium bowl, combine flour, baking powder; baking soda and salt; set aside.
2. In a large bowl, using an electric mixer, beat butter and sugar together until creamy.
3. Add eggs and vanilla to butter mixture, beat well. Add flour mixture alternately with sour cream, mixing just until the dry ingredients are moistened and a few lumps remain; fold in apples and pears.

4. Pour half of the batter into a greased 9x13-inch baking dish, sprinkle cinnamon sugar evenly across top, add remaining batter to baking dish.

5. Bake in a 350 degree oven for 35 minutes, or until a toothpick inserted in center comes out clean.

Serves: 12 – 15

BANANA MUFFINS

These muffins are so tender and light, I'll bet you can't eat just one.

2 cups all-purpose or light baking flour
½ teaspoon baking soda
2 teaspoons baking powder
½ teaspoon salt
1 teaspoon cinnamon
½ cup butter, softened
½ cup sugar
2 eggs
2 heaping tablespoons applesauce
1½ cups ripe bananas, mashed (about 3 bananas)
¼ cup orange juice
½ cup walnuts or pecans, finely ground (optional)

Heat oven to 375 degrees

1. In a medium bowl, combine flour, baking soda, baking powder, salt, and cinnamon; set aside.
2. In a large bowl, cream butter and sugar; add eggs.
3. Add applesauce, bananas, and orange juice, stirring until well combined.
4. Stir flour mixture into egg mixture, stirring just until the dry ingredients are moistened and a few lumps remain; fold in nuts if desired.
5. Spoon batter into greased muffin cups; bake at 375 degrees for 15-20 minutes, or until toothpick inserted in center comes out clean.
Yield: 12

BANANA PINEAPPLE BREAD

The pineapple gives this bread a very nice flavor. While pineapple is a rather chewy fruit, the crushed pineapple baked into this bread makes for an easy chew. However, if even crushed pineapple is difficult for you, just try one of the other delicious breads.

2 cups all-purpose or light baking flour
1 teaspoon baking soda
2 teaspoons baking powder
½ teaspoon salt
⅓ cup butter, softened
¼ cup applesauce
¼ cup granulated sugar
¼ cup brown sugar
2 eggs
1 cup banana, mashed
1 (8-ounce) can crushed pineapple, undrained

Heat oven to 350 degrees

1. In a medium bowl, combine flour, baking soda, baking powder, and salt; set aside.
2. Cream together butter, applesauce, and sugars; add eggs and mix well.
3. Add flour mixture to egg mixture, stirring just until the dry ingredients are moistened and a few lumps remain; fold in mashed banana and pineapple in juice.
4. Pour into a greased 9x5-inch loaf pan.
5. Bake at 350 degrees for 60 minutes, or until toothpick inserted in center comes out clean.
Yield: 1 loaf

BEET LOVERS LOAF

I came across this bread when I was in Australia and was intrigued to try it for myself. The beets give this bread a pink color, and ensure moistness, while the beet taste is subtle. Enjoy a slice with cream cheese on it.

2 cups all-purpose or light baking flour
3 teaspoons baking powder
½ cup granulated sugar
1 (15-ounce) can beets, drained, with ¼ cup liquid
   reserved
½ cup orange juice
2 tablespoons orange peel, grated
¼ cup vegetable oil
1 egg, lightly beaten
½ teaspoon vanilla

Heat oven to 350 degrees

1. In a large bowl, combine flour, baking powder and sugar; set aside.
2. Puree beets with ¼ cup reserved liquid in food processor or blender.
3. In a large bowl, add pureed beets, orange juice, grated orange peel, vegetable oil, egg and vanilla; combine well.
4. Add flour mixture to beet mixture, stirring just until the dry ingredients are moistened and a few lumps remain; pour into greased 9x5-inch loaf pan.
5. Bake at 350 degrees for 45 minutes, or until toothpick inserted in center comes out clean.
Yield: 1 loaf

BLUEBERRY MUFFINS

Blueberry muffins are an all-time favorite. Either fresh or frozen blueberries work beautifully, and feel free to add extra blueberries to make these muffins bursting with goodness.

1¾ cups all-purpose or light baking flour
⅓ cup sugar
2½ teaspoons baking powder
½ teaspoon salt
¾ cup milk
1 egg, lightly beaten
⅓ cup butter, softened
1 cup blueberries, fresh or frozen

Heat oven to 400 degrees

1. In a medium bowl, combine flour, sugar, baking powder, and salt; set aside.
2. In a large bowl, beat butter and sugar until creamy; add egg and milk.
3. Add flour mixture to butter mixture, stirring just until the dry ingredients are moistened and a few lumps remain; fold in blueberries.
4. Spoon batter into twelve greased muffin cups; bake at 400 degrees for 18 minutes, or until a toothpick inserted in center comes out clean.
Yield: 12

BOHEMIAN APPLE KOLACHES (KOLáCE)

I grew up with these delicious fruit filled rolls, made by hand by my grandmother, who grew up in a Bohemian community in Iowa.

2 packages active dry yeast
½ cup plus 1 tablespoon sugar
¼ cup lukewarm water
1¼ cups butter, divided, melted
2 cups milk
2 whole eggs plus 4 yolks
1 ½ teaspoons salt

½ teaspoon powdered lemon peel
1 teaspoon vanilla
6 – 7 cups flour

Apple Filling
2 cups applesauce
1 egg, beaten, reserved
cinnamon sugar

Heat oven to 400 degrees

1. Dissolve yeast in ¼ cup lukewarm water; add 1 tablespoon sugar, stir. Rest yeast mixture for 5 minutes or until bubbly.
2. Meanwhile, combine 1 cup melted butter and milk in the microwave or a saucepan until warmed (not scalding).
3. In a large bowl, add whole eggs and yolks plus remaining sugar and beat until thickened.
4. Add milk and butter mixture to egg mixture; beat in salt, lemon peel and vanilla.
5. Beat in flour, one cup at a time, until it becomes too thick to beat.

6. Place dough on floured pastry board and knead until smooth, about 5 minutes. Place in greased bowl, rounding up with greased side up. Cover with towel and let rise in a warm place until doubled.

7. Punch down dough; place on a lightly floured board and divide into 6 large pieces. Next cut each of the large pieces into 12 smaller pieces; form each into balls.

8. Place balls on a baking sheet and brush each with melted butter; cover and let rise again until double.

9. Press the center of each down, making a flat indentation in the center, and fill each with 1 tablespoon applesauce; let rise again, about 30 minutes.

10. Bake in a 400 degree oven for 7 to 10 minutes or just until lightly browned; sprinkle with cinnamon sugar.

Yield: 6 dozen

BUTTERMILK PRUNE MUFFINS

You can buy prunes that are already chopped into small bits, or you can use whole pitted prunes and cut them into small pieces. These tasty muffins are wonderful while still warm out of the oven. Try them with honey butter. Delicious.

2 cups water
1 cup prune bits
5 tablespoons butter, softened
3 tablespoons sugar
2 eggs, lightly beaten
1 cup buttermilk, room temperature
½ teaspoon salt
½ teaspoon lemon peel powder
½ teaspoon cinnamon
¾ cup whole wheat flour
1¼ cup all-purpose or light baking flour
1 tablespoon baking powder
½ teaspoon baking soda

Heat oven to 400 degrees

1. In a small saucepan, boil water; remove from heat. Add prunes and let soak for 8 minutes. Drain prunes; sift some of the flour over the prune bits; toss to coat, then set aside.
2. In a large bowl, cream butter and sugar; add eggs and buttermilk.

3. Add salt, lemon powder, cinnamon, flours, baking powder and baking soda, mixing just until the dry ingredients are moistened and a few lumps remain; fold in prunes.

4. Spoon batter into greased muffin cups; bake at 400 degrees for 18 minutes, or until toothpick inserted in center comes out clean.

Yield: 12

CHEESY CHIVE MUFFINS

This is a savory muffin, rather than the common sweet muffin. I make these tasty morsels to eat with light, blended soups, such as tomato or zucchini-potato soup. Need that sweet taste? Try a little honey butter on them.

2 cups all-purpose or light baking flour
1 teaspoon salt
3 teaspoons baking powder
½ teaspoon paprika
2 eggs, lightly beaten
1 cup buttermilk
¾ cup milk
½ cup cheddar cheese, shredded
½ cup Parmesan cheese, grated
½ cup vegetable oil
3 tablespoons chives, finely chopped

Heat oven to 350 degrees

1. In a large bowl, mix flour, salt, baking powder and paprika; set aside.
2. In a medium bowl, add eggs, buttermilk, milk, cheddar cheese, Parmesan cheese and oil; mix well.
3. Pour egg mixture into flour mixture, stirring just until the dry ingredients are moistened and a few lumps remain; stir in chives.
4. Spoon into greased muffin cups; bake in a 350 degree oven for 15 minutes, or until toothpick inserted in center comes out clean.
Yield: 12

CHEESY-CHINI MUFFINS

These delicious savory muffins are amazingly light and tender. Be sure to use a whisk when blending as whisking helps make these tasty treats so light.

2 cups all-purpose or light baking flour
1½ teaspoons baking powder
½ teaspoon baking soda
3 tablespoons sugar
½ teaspoon salt
2 eggs, lightly beaten
1¼ cups buttermilk
½ cup butter, melted
1 cup zucchini, shredded
¾ cup cheddar cheese, shredded

Heat oven to 400 degrees

1. In a large bowl, combine flour, baking powder, baking soda, sugar and salt; set aside.
2. In a medium bowl, whisk together eggs and buttermilk; whisk in melted butter.
3. Add egg mixture to flour mixture; whisk just until dry ingredients are moistened and a few lumps remain; fold in zucchini and cheddar cheese.
4. Spoon batter into greased muffin cups; bake at 400 degrees for 18 minutes, or until a toothpick inserted in center comes out clean.
Yield: 12

CORNBREAD

Cornbread is an excellent accompaniment to many types of dishes, from soups and salads to bean dishes.

1 cup all-purpose or light baking flour
1 cup yellow cornmeal, finely ground
¼ cup sugar
2 teaspoons baking powder
½ teaspoon baking soda
½ teaspoon salt
1 egg
⅓ cup applesauce
2 tablespoons butter, melted
1 cup buttermilk or milk

Heat oven to 425 degrees

1. In a medium bowl, combine flour, cornmeal, sugar, baking powder, baking soda and salt; set aside.
2. In a large bowl, add egg, applesauce and butter; mix well.
3. Add flour mixture alternately with buttermilk or milk to egg mixture, mixing just until the dry ingredients are moistened and a few lumps remain.
4. Pour batter into a greased 9x9-inch baking dish; bake at 425 degrees for 18 minutes, or until toothpick inserted in center comes out clean.
Serves: 9 – 12

CRANBERRY COFFEE CAKE

Rich and delicious, this coffee cake is wonderful for a special occasion. You can use cherry pie filling instead of cranberry sauce, or another fruit pie filling of your choice.

2 cups all-purpose or light baking flour
1 teaspoon baking powder
1 teaspoon baking soda
½ teaspoon salt
½ cup butter, softened
1 cup sugar
2 eggs
1 teaspoon vanilla
1 cup sour cream
1 (16-ounce) can whole cranberry sauce
powdered sugar or icing (page 253)

Heat oven to 350 degrees

1. In a medium bowl, combine flour, baking powder, baking soda and salt; set aside.
2. In a large bowl, beat butter and sugar together until fluffy; add eggs and vanilla, beating until smooth.
3. Add flour mixture to egg mixture alternately with sour cream, mixing just until the dry ingredients are moistened and a few lumps remain.
4. Pour half of the batter into a greased 9x13-inch baking dish.
5. Spoon half of the cranberry sauce over the batter; top with remaining batter, then spoon remaining cranberry

sauce evenly across top. Bake in a 350 degree oven for 45 minutes, or until a toothpick inserted in center comes out clean.

6. Cool; dust with powdered sugar, or drizzle with icing if preferred.

Serves: 12 – 15

MINIATURE APPLESAUCE MUFFINS

These miniature muffins are the perfect size for those with small appetites – one or two on the side will be so tempting to eat.

2 cups all-purpose or light baking flour
1 teaspoon baking soda
⅛ teaspoon baking powder
1 teaspoon cinnamon
¼ teaspoon cloves
¼ teaspoon nutmeg
¼ teaspoon salt
½ cup butter, softened
¾ cup sugar
1 egg, lightly beaten
1¼ cups applesauce

Heat oven to 350 degrees

1. In a medium bowl, combine flour, baking soda, baking powder, cinnamon, cloves, nutmeg and salt; set aside.
2. In a large bowl, beat butter and sugar until smooth; add egg, continue beating. Stir in applesauce.
3. Add flour mixture to butter mixture, stirring just until the dry ingredients are moistened and a few lumps remain.
4. Spoon batter into greased mini-muffin pans; bake in a 350 degree oven for 12-14 minutes, or until toothpick inserted in center comes out clean.

Yield: 36

MOIST BRAN MUFFINS

*These delicious muffins are wonderfully moist and soft.
Just be sure not to over-bake them. They freeze well, too.*

1½ cups all-bran cereal
1 cup milk
2 eggs
½ cup applesauce
½ cup brown sugar
½ cup vegetable oil
1 cup all-purpose or light baking flour
1½ teaspoon baking powder
½ teaspoon baking soda
¼ teaspoon salt
½ cup diced pears (optional)
½ cup raisins, plumper & moister style (optional)

Heat oven to 400 degrees

1. In a small bowl, combine bran and milk; let soak for 10 minutes to soften.
2. Meanwhile, in a medium bowl, beat together eggs, applesauce, sugar and oil.
3. Add bran mixture to egg mixture and stir together; add flour, baking powder, baking soda and salt, stirring just until the dry ingredients are moistened and a few lumps remain. Fold in pears and/or raisins if desired.
4. Spoon batter into 12 greased muffin cups; bake at 400 degrees for 15 minutes, or until toothpick inserted in center comes out clean.
Yield: 12

MORNING GLORY MUFFINS

My all-time favorite, I make them over and over again. I often eat them with cottage cheese for a quick and nutritious breakfast or for a light lunch.

2 cups all-purpose or light baking flour
2 teaspoons baking soda
½ teaspoon baking powder
2 teaspoons cinnamon
¼ teaspoon salt
½ cup granulated sugar
½ cup brown sugar
1 cup vegetable oil
3 eggs, lightly beaten
2 teaspoons vanilla
2 cups carrots, peeled and shredded
1 medium cooking apple, peeled and grated
½ cup walnuts, finely ground (optional)
½ cup raisins, moister & plumper style (optional)

Heat oven to 350 degrees

1. In a medium bowl, combine flour, baking soda, baking powder, cinnamon and salt; set aside.
2. In a large bowl, combine sugars and oil; add eggs and vanilla. Mix well.
3. Stir flour mixture into egg mixture, stirring just until the dry ingredients are moistened and a few lumps remain; fold in carrots and apple, plus walnuts and raisins if desired.

4. Spoon batter into greased muffin cups; bake at 350 degrees for 20 minutes, or until a toothpick inserted in center comes out clean.

Yield: 15

PEACH COFFEE CAKE

This coffee cake has been a favorite of my family's for decades. The recipe can be easily doubled and baked in a 9x13-inch baking dish. You may want seconds of this one!

1½ cups all-purpose or light baking flour
½ teaspoon baking soda
 2 teaspoons baking powder
¼ cup butter, softened
⅓ cup applesauce
½ cup sugar
1 egg
½ cup milk
1½ cups peaches, sliced or diced
cinnamon sugar or powdered sugar

Heat oven to 350 degrees

1. In a medium bowl, combine flour, baking soda and baking powder; set aside.
2. In a large bowl, using an electric mixer, beat butter, applesauce and half cup sugar until light and fluffy; add egg, mixing well.
3. Add flour mixture alternately with milk to egg mixture; mixing just until the dry ingredients are moistened and a few lumps remain.
4. Pour batter into greased 8x8-inch baking dish; spread peaches over the top, pushing down slightly into the batter.

5. Bake in a 350 degree oven for 30 minutes, or until a toothpick inserted in center comes out clean.

6. Cool; sprinkle with cinnamon sugar or dust with powdered sugar.

Serves: 10 – 12

PUMPKIN-BANANA BREAD

This pumpkin bread is so moist and flavorful you won't be able to resist having that second slice.

1¾ cups all-purpose or light baking flour
1½ teaspoons baking powder
½ teaspoon baking soda
1 teaspoon cinnamon
¼ teaspoon allspice
½ teaspoon ground ginger
½ teaspoon salt
½ cup oil
½ cup granulated sugar
¼ cup brown sugar
1 medium ripe banana, mashed
¾ cup pumpkin puree
2 eggs, lightly beaten
1 tablespoon orange juice
1 heaping teaspoon grated orange peel

Heat oven to 350 degrees

1. In a medium bowl, combine flour, baking powder, baking soda, cinnamon, allspice, ginger and salt; set aside.
2. In a large bowl, stir oil and sugars together until well blended.
3. Add banana, pumpkin, eggs, orange juice, and orange peel; mix well.

4. Add flour mixture to banana mixture, mixing just until the dry ingredients are moistened and a few lumps remain.

5. Pour into greased bread pan; bake in a 350 degree oven for 1 hour, or until a toothpick inserted in center comes out clean

Yield: 1 loaf

Quick and Cheesy Corn Muffins

These muffins are quick to make, and always come out great. You can easily double this recipe to make corn bread instead of the individual muffins. I sometimes puree cottage cheese and use that instead of the cheddar cheese. These are a perfect for anyone needing extra protein in their diet.

1 (8½-ounce) package corn muffin mix
2 heaping tablespoons applesauce
½ cup cheddar cheese, shredded

Heat oven to 400 degrees

1. In a medium bowl, make corn muffin mix according to package directions, stir in the applesauce.
2. Fold in cheddar cheese; spoon into greased muffins cups.
3. Bake at 400 degrees for 15 minutes, or until toothpick inserted in center comes out clean.
Yield: 6 – 8

SWEET POTATO MUFFINS

I fell in love with these muffins the first time I made them. This is definitely a recipe to make over and over again.

1¾ cups all-purpose or light baking flour
¾ cup sugar
1½ teaspoon cinnamon
½ teaspoon nutmeg
½ teaspoon baking soda
¾ teaspoon baking powder
½ teaspoon salt
2 eggs, lightly beaten
1 cup sweet potatoes, cooked and mashed
½ cup vegetable oil
¼ cup applesauce
⅓ cup water

Heat oven to 350 degrees

1. In a large bowl, combine flour, sugar, cinnamon, nutmeg, baking soda, baking powder, and salt; set aside.
2. In a small bowl, mix eggs, sweet potatoes, oil, applesauce, and water.
3. Stir sweet potato mixture into flour mixture, stirring just until the dry ingredients are moistened and a few lumps remain.
4. Spoon batter into greased muffin cups; bake at 350 degrees for 18 minutes, or until a toothpick inserted in center comes out clean.
Yield: 12

Zucchini Bread

Zucchini adds luscious moisture to any baked good. Be sure not to over-bake so the bread will retain its moisture.

3 cups all-purpose or light baking flour
¾ teaspoon salt
1 teaspoon baking soda
1½ teaspoons baking powder
2 teaspoons cinnamon
1 cup sugar
¾ cup vegetable oil
¼ cup applesauce
3 eggs, lightly beaten
2 teaspoons vanilla
2½ cups zucchini, shredded
½ cup walnuts, finely ground (optional)
½ cup raisins, plump and moist style (optional)

Heat oven to 325 degrees

1. In a medium bowl, combine flour, salt, baking soda, baking powder and cinnamon; set aside.
2. In a large bowl, combine sugar, oil, applesauce, eggs and vanilla; beat well.
3. Stir flour mixture into egg mixture, stirring just until the dry ingredients are moistened and a few lumps remain; fold in shredded zucchini, plus walnuts and raisins if desired.

4. Pour batter into two greased 9 x 5-inch loaf pans; bake in a 325 degree oven for 35–40 minutes, or until a toothpick inserted in center comes out clean.

Yield: 2 loaves

BREAKFAST

BANANA PANCAKES

These pancakes will have everyone coming back for more. You may need to double the recipe! I sometimes make them ahead and keep them in the freezer to reheat for a quick meal along with a scrambled egg.

1 medium to large banana, very ripe
1 large egg, lightly beaten
1 cup milk
1 cup all-purpose or light baking flour
1 tablespoon baking powder
1 tablespoon vegetable oil
1 tablespoon brown sugar
1/8 teaspoon salt
1/4 teaspoon cinnamon

1. In a medium bowl, mash banana. Add egg and milk; stir to combine.
2. Add flour, baking powder, oil, brown sugar, salt, and cinnamon, whisking just until the dry ingredients are moistened and a few lumps remain.
3. Pour or spoon batter into buttered skillet to make pancakes; when bubbles begin to form, and the underside is browned, turn over to brown other side. Remove cooked pancakes and repeat process with remaining batter.
Serves: 4

BREAKFAST FRITTATA

An "anytime" meal that goes from stovetop to oven to serving table in the same skillet. If you prefer, you can use ground ham in this recipe instead of sausage.

3 tablespoons vegetable oil
2 cups diced frozen hash browns, thawed
½ pound bulk sausage
1 small onion, finely chopped
1 small green pepper, finely chopped
6 eggs, separated
¼ cup milk
½ teaspoon salt
½ teaspoon black pepper
½ cup Cheddar cheese, shredded

Heat oven to 350 degrees.

1. In a large oven proof skillet, heat oil over medium heat; add potatoes, stir until tender and lightly browned. Transfer potatoes to a bowl.
2. Place sausage, onion, and green pepper in the skillet; cook over medium heat, stirring until vegetables are softened and sausage is browned and crumbly. Drain fat.
3. Remove skillet from heat; return potatoes to skillet, stirring to combine potatoes and sausage mixture.
4. In a medium bowl, beat egg whites until stiff.
5. In a large bowl, beat egg yolks until thick and lemon colored; beat in milk, salt and pepper. Gently fold egg whites into egg yolks.

6. Pour eggs over sausage mixture; gently combine. Cover; cook over low heat for 10 minutes to set eggs.

7. Uncover, sprinkle with cheese, and place uncovered frittata in a 350 degree oven for 10 minutes and cheese is melted and eggs are set.

Serves: 4

Breakfast Sausage Sandwich

A sausage lover's delight. This sandwich can be taken to eat on the run or part of a formal sit down brunch and eaten with a knife and fork.

12-ounces bulk pork sausage
¼ cup green bell pepper, finely chopped
1 clove garlic, finely chopped
1 (3-ounce) package cream cheese, softened
1 tablespoon fresh parsley, finely chopped
1 (8-ounce) tube refrigerated crescent rolls

Heat oven to 350 degrees

1. In a medium skillet, cook sausage, bell pepper, and garlic over medium heat; stir until sausage is browned and crumbly. Drain fat.
2. Add cream cheese and stir over low heat until cheese melts; add parsley.
3. Remove crescent rolls from tube; separate along perforations into 8 separate triangles; place 1-inch apart on baking sheet.
4. Spoon sausage mixture onto center of each triangle, dividing evenly among all 8 triangles; fold each tip of the triangle over the sausage mixture, tuck under and seal together.
5. Bake at 350 degrees for 15 minutes, or until golden brown.
Serves: 8

BUTTERMILK PANCAKES

The beaten egg whites give these pancakes a light texture. If you like, sprinkle blueberries on top of the batter while cooking, or cooked chopped apples, for added flavor and nutrition.

¼ cup butter, softened
2 cups buttermilk
2 large eggs, separated
1½ cups all-purpose or light baking flour
1½ tablespoons sugar
½ teaspoon salt
1½ teaspoons baking powder
1 teaspoon baking soda

1. In a large bowl, beat together butter, buttermilk and egg yolk.
2. Add flour, sugar, salt, baking powder, and baking soda, stirring just until the dry ingredients are moistened and a few lumps remain
3. In a separate bowl, beat egg whites until frothy and slightly stiffened; gently fold the egg whites into the batter.
4. Pour or spoon batter into buttered skillet to make pancakes; when bubbles begin to form, and the underside is browned, turn over to brown other side. Remove cooked pancakes and repeat process with remaining batter.
Serves: 4 – 6

CHEESY GRITS

Easy to make, and packed full of both flavor and protein. When my mother asked for seconds I knew it was a winner.

1 cup grits, uncooked
3 eggs, lightly beaten
1 cup cheddar cheese, shredded
¼ cup half-and-half

1. Prepare the grits according to the package directions.

2. Meanwhile, in a small bowl, combine the beaten eggs with the cheese.

3. When the grits are almost done, stir 3 tablespoons of the hot grits into the egg mixture.

4. Add the egg mixture to the cooking grits; whisk the egg mixture into the grits until the grits are smooth.

5. Add half-and-half; continue whisking until the grits are of desired consistency.

Serves: 6

CHEESY TOMATO OMELET

An omelet is simple to make, soft to eat, and oh so versatile a dish. You can add finely chopped shaved ham, cooked green or red peppers, or any soft combination you like.

½ teaspoon butter
1 large egg
1 tablespoon milk or water
salt to taste
black pepper to taste
garlic powder to taste
1 slice cheddar cheese
1 tablespoon tomato, peeled and finely chopped

1. In a 6-inch nonstick skillet, melt butter over medium heat; turn skillet to coat evenly.
2. In a small bowl, whisk egg and milk or water; pour into skillet. Sprinkle salt, pepper and garlic powder over top of egg.
3. When edges of egg mixture begin to cook, lift edges with a spatula and tip the skillet so uncooked egg flows underneath to cook.
4. Continue to do step 3 until top is almost dry. Place cheese slice on top, then the tomatoes over half of the omelet.
5. When cheese begins to melt, fold in half and serve.
Serves: 1

Colorful Scrambled Eggs

These eggs have good flavor and nice color. With the red of the bell pepper and the green of the chives this is a cheerful dish during the holiday season.

4 eggs
⅛ teaspoon salt
⅛ teaspoon pepper
2 tablespoons olive oil
2 tablespoons red bell pepper, finely chopped
1 clove garlic, finely chopped
1½ teaspoons chives, finely chopped

1. In a medium bowl, beat together eggs, salt and pepper; set aside.
2. In a large skillet, heat oil; add red bell pepper and garlic. Cook over medium heat, stirring until softened, about 5 minutes.
3. Add egg mixture and chives to skillet; cook and stir over low heat until eggs are cooked.
Serves: 2 - 4

CORN MEAL MUSH WITH POLISH SAUSAGE

Mush is a familiar food in the Midwest, and this comfort food is sure to please. My parents like the flavor of Polish sausage with mush, and a fried or scrambled egg goes well with it too.

1 (16-ounce) package refrigerated corn meal mush
½ (16-ounce) package skinless Polish sausage
½ tablespoon butter
maple syrup

1. Cut both mush and sausage into 1-inch slices; set aside.
2. In a large skillet, melt butter over medium heat; add mush, laying slices side by side. Cook until softened and lightly browned on one side, about 10 minutes; turn over to brown other side.
3. After turning mush over to brown other side, add sausage to skillet; place around edges of skillet and between mush slices to warm throughout (you may also use a separate skillet to heat sausage).
4. Serve with maple syrup drizzled on top.
Serves: 2 – 4

CORNED BEEF HASH

This recipe calls for canned corned beef because it is so soft, however you can use corned beef that you have cooked if you chop it fine, being sure to remove any tough pieces.

3 tablespoons butter
1 cup onion, finely chopped
½ cup green cabbage, finely chopped
1 (12-ounce) can cooked corned beef, finely chopped
3 cups frozen diced hash brown potatoes, thawed and
  drained
salt and pepper to taste

1. In a large skillet, melt butter; add onion and cabbage and cook until vegetables become softened, about 10 minutes; add a little water if needed.

2. Add the corned beef, hash browns, salt and pepper; mix well, and spread mixture evenly over bottom of skillet to ensure even cooking.

3. Press down on the hash with a spatula and allow it to cook without stirring until you hear it begin to sizzle, as you want it to brown.

4. When one side is browned, flip over with spatula to brown the other side.

5. When both sides are browned, remove from heat and serve.

Serves: 4 - 6

Cottage Cheese Pancakes

The cottage cheese makes these pancakes moist and packs in the protein. Don't expect them to be as fluffy as your box mix pancakes. They are deliciously different and go well with traditional maple syrup topping or fresh fruit. If you prefer a thinner batter, add more milk.

1 cup cottage cheese
3 eggs
½ cup milk
1 cup all-purpose or light baking flour
2 tablespoons sugar
1 teaspoon baking power

1. Place cottage cheese, eggs and milk in a blender; blend until smooth.
2. Add flour, sugar and baking powder to blender, blending just until the dry ingredients are moistened and a few lumps remain.
3. Pour or spoon batter into a buttered skillet to make pancakes; when bubbles begin to form, and the underside is browned, turn over to brown other side.
4. Remove cooked pancakes and repeat process with remaining batter.
Serves: 6

CREAMED EGGS ON TOAST

This traditional recipe for creamed eggs on toast can be spiced up by adding a dash of onion powder, garlic powder, curry powder, or mustard powder. Baking powder biscuits can make a nice change from the traditional toast, too.

1 tablespoon butter
1½ tablespoons all-purpose flour
¼ teaspoon salt
1 cup milk
4 large hard-cooked eggs, peeled and chopped
4 slices of soft bread, lightly toasted
paprika (optional)

1. In a small saucepan, melt butter over low heat; add flour and salt, stirring until smooth.
2. Gradually add milk to saucepan, stirring continuously until thickened to desired consistency and creaminess.
3. Remove from heat; stir in chopped eggs, allow to stand a minute to heat eggs through, then spoon over toast. Sprinkle with paprika before serving if desired.

Serves: 2 – 4

DUTCH PANCAKES

A light and enjoyable dish. Use your favorite soft fruit as a topping, and you might try skipping the sugar on top and add a large dollop of vanilla yogurt instead.

2 tablespoons butter
3 eggs
½ cup milk
½ cup all-purpose or light baking flour
dash of salt
¼ teaspoon nutmeg or cinnamon
1 cup fresh strawberries, sliced
powdered sugar

Heat oven to 425 degrees

1. Place butter in a 10-inch glass pie plate; put pie plate in preheated oven until the butter is melted.
2. Meanwhile, in a medium bowl, whisk eggs and milk together.
3. Add flour, nutmeg or cinnamon, and salt; whisk just until smooth.
4. Pour batter into buttery pie plate; bake at 425 degrees for 20 minutes, or until puffed up.
5. Remove from oven, cut in half, place on plates and top with fresh strawberry slices; sprinkle with powdered sugar.
Serves: 2

EGGS WITH MUSHROOMS

For variety, you can easily replace the mushrooms in this dish with another soft vegetable such as diced tomatoes or chopped fresh spinach. Use your favorite soft vegetable to make your own creation.

1 teaspoon butter
½ cup fresh mushrooms, finely chopped
⅛ teaspoon salt
1 tablespoon milk
2 eggs, lightly beaten
pepper to taste

1. In a small pan, melt butter; add mushrooms and salt, cooking until mushrooms are soft and liquid evaporates.
2. In a small bowl, whisk milk, eggs, and pepper.
3. Pour egg mixture over mushrooms and scramble together until cooked through.
Serves: 2

FRENCH TOAST CASSEROLE

A wonderful make-ahead dish. You can either place it in the refrigerator overnight to enjoy for breakfast, or put it together first thing in the morning to bake later for a light supper. Easy to make, and it can be easier yet if you ask the bakery to cut the bread into 1-inch slices for you. Serve with fresh fruit slices, if desired.

½ pound French or Vienna bread (about ½ of a long loaf)
8 eggs, lightly beaten
3 cups milk
4 teaspoons sugar
1 teaspoon cinnamon
¼ teaspoon salt
1 teaspoon vanilla
2 tablespoons butter (reserved)
1 teaspoon grated orange peel (optional)
¼ teaspoon nutmeg (optional)
maple syrup

Heat oven to 350 degrees

1. Slice bread into 1-inch slices; remove crusts.

2. Place the bread slices in a single layer in the bottom of a 9x13-inch greased baking dish.

3. In a medium bowl, beat or whisk together eggs, milk, sugar, salt, vanilla, and cinnamon, plus orange peel and nutmeg if desired.

4. Pour the egg mixture over the bread slices; cover tightly and refrigerate overnight.

5. Before baking, cut the 2 tablespoons of butter into small pieces and place on top of bread slices.

6. Bake uncovered in a 350 degree oven for 30-35 minutes, or until puffy and lightly browned.

7. Serve with maple syrup.

Serves: 6 - 8

HAM & EGGS QUICHE

In my family, seconds are always requested with this quiche—it turns out looking great and tasting wonderful.

1 pie crust, unbaked deep dish
2 (5-ounce) cans ground smoked ham, crumbled
½ cup fresh mushrooms, sliced or finely chopped
½ cup onion, finely chopped
¼ cup green pepper, finely chopped
1 teaspoon parsley flakes
1 teaspoon garlic powder
salt and pepper to taste
1 tablespoon all-purpose flour
1 cup Monterey Jack or Cheddar cheese, shredded
1 cup milk
2 eggs, lightly beaten

Heat oven to 325 degrees

1. In a medium bowl combine ham, mushrooms, onion, green pepper, parsley flakes, garlic powder, salt and pepper.
2. Pour ham mixture into pie crust. Sprinkle with flour, then with cheese.
3. In a medium bowl, add milk and eggs; beat or whisk until smooth.
4. Pour egg mixture slowly into the pie over the top of the cheese.
5. Bake in a 325 degree oven for 50 minutes, or until knife inserted in center comes out clean.
Serves: 6

HASH BROWN AND EGGS SKILLET

This easy-to-make one skillet dish is one of our family favorites for a quick meal any time of day. Get out the catsup and enjoy!

¼ cup vegetable oil
½ cup onion, finely chopped
½ cup green or red pepper, finely chopped
1 (16-ounce) package frozen diced hash brown potatoes, thawed
⅓ cup water
1 tablespoon garlic powder
6 eggs, lightly beaten
1 teaspoon salt
½ teaspoon black pepper
½ cup cheddar cheese, shredded (optional)

1. In a large skillet, heat oil over medium heat; add onions and green or red pepper; stir and cook until softened.
2. Add hash browns, water, and garlic powder; mix well. Cover; cook over low heat about 15-20 minutes, until hash browns are softened.
3. Uncover hash browns; continue cooking over medium heat, occasionally turning hash browns to lightly brown.
4. Meanwhile, in a medium bowl, whisk eggs.
5. When hash browns are lightly browned, pour eggs on top; add salt and pepper.
6. Stir frequently, until eggs are cooked and well combined with hash browns.
7. Before serving, sprinkle cheese on top if desired.

Serves: 6

PUMPKIN PANCAKES

The pumpkin makes these pancakes light and moist. They have a subtle pumpkin flavor with just enough pumpkin to be able to taste and enjoy. If you have pumpkin pie spice on hand, you can replace the last three spices in this recipe with that instead. Top with homemade applesauce and maple syrup – delicious!

1 large egg, beaten
¼ cup vanilla yogurt
¾ cup milk
¾ cup canned pumpkin
2 tablespoons butter, melted
1 cup all-purpose or light baking flour
¼ teaspoon salt
2 tablespoons brown sugar
2 teaspoons baking powder
½ teaspoon baking soda
½ teaspoon cinnamon
¼ teaspoon nutmeg
½ teaspoon powdered ginger

1. In a large bowl, combine egg, yogurt, milk, pumpkin, and melted butter, mix well.
2. Add flour, salt, sugar, baking powder, baking soda, and spices; stir or whisk just until the dry ingredients are moistened and a few lumps remain.
3. Pour or spoon batter into buttered skillet to make pancakes; when bubbles begin to form, and the underside is browned, turn over to brown other side. Remove cooked pancakes and repeat process with remaining batter.
Serves: 4

SAUSAGE AND EGG "PIZZA"

Don't despair over the way it looks when putting it into the oven – it turns out great. You can substitute ground ham for the sausage, if preferred, or add the topping of your choice.

1 pound bulk sausage
1 (8-ounce) tube refrigerated crescent rolls
1 cup frozen hash brown potatoes, thawed and drained
1 cup cheddar cheese, shredded
4 eggs
¼ cup milk
½ teaspoon salt
¼ teaspoon black pepper
¼ cup Parmesan cheese, grated (optional)

Heat oven to 375 degrees

1. In a medium skillet, cook sausage over medium heat; stir until sausage is browned and crumbly. Drain fat.

2. Remove crescent rolls from package and place evenly around a 9-inch pizza pan; pinch seams together to form the pizza crust.

3. Spoon the sausage over the top of the pizza dough; top with potatoes and cheddar cheese.

4. In a medium bowl, whisk eggs, milk, salt and pepper; gently pour over the top of the sausage mixture. Sprinkle with Parmesan cheese if desired.

5. Bake in a 375 degree oven for 20–25 minutes.

Serves: 4 - 6

SAUSAGE GRAVY AND BISCUITS

This is a good old fashioned, tried-and-true recipe for sausage gravy. In this case, simple is indeed good!

8-ounces bulk pork sausage
¼ cup all-purpose flour
2 cups milk
½ teaspoon salt
½ teaspoon black pepper
4 soft baking powder biscuits

1. In a medium skillet, cook sausage over medium heat; stir until sausage is browned and crumbly. Drain fat, reserving 1 tablespoon in skillet. Set sausage aside.
2. Add flour to skillet, stirring until smooth.
3. Over medium heat, gradually add milk to skillet, stirring until of desired thickness; stir in sausage, salt and pepper.
4. Break biscuits into halves and place on serving plates; spoon sausage gravy over tops of biscuits.
Serves: 2 – 4

SCRAMBLED EGGS AND RICE

You don't have to eat the same old eggs and toast for breakfast. This dish is deliciously different. If you have some fresh mushrooms on hand, slice a few and toss them in to cook with the onions.

2 teaspoons butter
1 tablespoon green onions, finely chopped
3 eggs, lightly beaten
1 tablespoon milk
1 cup white or brown rice, cooked
1 teaspoon pimentos, finely chopped
salt and pepper to taste

1. In a medium skillet, melt butter; add onions and cook until softened.
2. In a medium bowl, add eggs and milk; whisk until smooth.
3. Add egg mixture to skillet; scramble until almost done.
4. Stir in cooked rice, pimentos, salt, and pepper; continue stirring until eggs are done and ingredients are heated throughout.
Serves: 2

Slow Cooker Apple Oatmeal

This breakfast is a time saver in the morning. It is prepared the night before and ready and waiting for you when you get up. I've made it with fresh peaches instead of apples and it turned out great. If you like sweeter oatmeal, you can substitute more apple juice for the water, or just add more brown sugar.

4 cups oatmeal
2 cups apple juice
4½ cups water
2 teaspoons cinnamon
¼ cup brown sugar
2 apples, peeled and chopped

1. In a slow cooker, add oatmeal, apple juice, water, cinnamon, and sugar. Mix well.
2. Add apples evenly across top; push down into oatmeal.
3. Cover; cook on low for 8 hours, or overnight.
Serves: 6 – 8

STOVETOP

BEEF STROGANOFF

A classic beef and noodle dish made with ground beef in place of beef strips, but just as enjoyable.

1 (8-ounce) package egg noodles
1 pound lean ground beef
½ cup onion, finely chopped
2 cloves garlic, thinly sliced
½ pound fresh mushrooms, thinly sliced or finely chopped
1 (14-ounce) can beef broth, divided
1 (.87-ounce) package beef gravy
1 cup sour cream

1. Cook noodles according to package instructions.

2. In a large skillet, cook ground beef, onion, and garlic, stirring until ground beef is browned and crumbly and onions are softened. Drain fat.

3. Add mushrooms and ½ cup broth; cook over low heat until softened, about 10 minutes, stirring often.

4. Cover; cook over low heat 10 minutes to further soften.

5. In a small bowl, combine gravy mix and remaining broth; pour into skillet, stir until near boiling and thickened.

6. Stir in sour cream and continue cooking until heated throughout. Serve over hot noodles.

Serves: 4 – 6

CHEESE RAVIOLI WITH BROCCOLI SAUCE

The broccoli lover will especially enjoy this dish. While this recipe leaves some of the cooked broccoli florets unblended, the entire broccoli sauce can be easily blended for a totally smooth and creamy sauce.

2 tablespoons olive oil
2 cloves garlic, finely chopped
1 cup chicken broth
1 (16-ounce) package frozen broccoli florets
1 (9-ounce) package refrigerated cheese ravioli
1 cup half-and-half
dash of nutmeg
½ teaspoon salt
¼ teaspoon black pepper
½ cup Parmesan cheese, grated (optional)

1. In a large skillet, heat olive oil; add garlic and cook over low heat until softened, about 3 minutes.

2. Add broth and broccoli; cover and cook over low heat until broccoli is very tender.

3. Meanwhile, cook ravioli according to package directions; drain and set aside.

4. Remove broccoli mixture from heat; transfer two-thirds of the broccoli mixture to a blender. Blend until smooth and return to skillet.

5. Add half and half, nutmeg, salt and pepper; stir.

6. Add ravioli to the skillet; toss, and continue cooking until heated throughout. Sprinkle with Parmesan cheese before serving if desired.

Serves: 4

CHEESE TORTELLINI WITH MEAT SAUCE

One pot cooking makes this dish a breeze to make. You can substitute ravioli for the tortellini, if preferred.

½ pound ground beef
¼ cup onion, finely chopped
2 cloves garlic, finely chopped
1 (14-ounce) jar spaghetti sauce
1½ cups water
1 (9-ounce) package cheese filled tortellini
½ cup Mozzarella cheese, shredded

1. In a large skillet, cook ground beef, onion, and garlic; break beef apart with spoon as it cooks, until it becomes browned and crumbly. Drain fat.

2. Add spaghetti sauce and water; bring to near boiling.

3. Stir in tortellini; cover and cook over low heat for 20 minutes, or until tender.

4. Sprinkle with Mozzarella cheese before serving.

Serves: 4

CHICKEN AND DUMPLINGS

This dish takes a few extra steps and minutes to make, but is well worth the effort. It is absolutely delicious.

2½ pounds chicken breasts or thighs
2 (14½-ounce) cans chicken broth
½ cup water
1½ cups onion, chopped, divided
2 stalks of celery, quartered
1 cup carrots, thinly sliced
1 cup green beans
½ cup peas

1 teaspoon celery seeds
½ teaspoon white pepper
1 tablespoon parsley flakes
¾ teaspoon poultry seasoning
1 tablespoon cornstarch
⅛ cup water

Dumplings
2 cups baking mix
⅔ cup milk

1. In a large saucepan, add chicken, broth, water, ¾ cup onion, and celery; bring to near boiling then reduce heat. Cover; cook over low heat for 50 minutes, or until chicken is tender.

2. Remove chicken; cool slightly and cut into bite-size pieces.

3. Strain the broth to remove fat, onion, and celery. Return broth to saucepan.

4. Add chicken pieces, carrots, green beans, peas, celery seeds, pepper, parsley, and poultry seasoning.

5. Cover; cook over low heat for 45 minutes, or until vegetables are tender.

6. In a small bowl, mix cornstarch and water; stir into chicken and vegetables.

7. In a medium bowl combine baking mix and milk.

8. Place spoonfuls of the dumpling mixture on top of hot stew. Cover and simmer for 12-15 minutes, or until dumplings are cooked through.

Serves: 4 – 6

CHICKEN AND NOODLES

By using at least one cup of homemade chicken broth from cooking the chicken you will add wonderfully to the flavor of this soft dish.

2 tablespoons vegetable oil
½ cup carrots, shredded
½ cup onion, finely chopped
2 cloves garlic, sliced
1½ cups cooked chicken, finely chopped
2 cups chicken broth
1 cup water
1 teaspoon seasoned salt
½ teaspoon black pepper
½ teaspoon basil
1 (8-ounce) package egg noodles, uncooked

1. In a large skillet, heat oil; add carrots, onions and garlic. Cook over low heat until softened, about 5 minutes.
2. Add chicken, broth, water, seasoned salt, pepper, and basil; heat until nearly boiling. Add noodles, stir.
3. Cover; cook over low heat for 30 minutes, or until vegetables and noodles are tender, stirring occasionally.
Serves: 4 – 6

CHICKEN AND RICE

I've made this dish more times than I can count. It's simple, tasty and filling. And it's good for you too! Add any of your favorite soft vegetables, being sure to increase the amount of broth if you add lots of veggies.

2 tablespoons butter or olive oil
½ cup onion, finely chopped
½ cup carrots, shredded
1 cup white rice, uncooked
1¼ cups chicken broth
1 cup water
1 cup cooked chicken, finely chopped
1 teaspoon seasoned salt

1. In a medium saucepan, melt butter over medium heat; add onions and carrots; cook and stir until softened, about 5 minutes.
2. Stir in rice, broth, water, chicken and seasoned salt.
3. Cover, cook over low heat, stirring occasionally, until liquid is absorbed and rice is tender, about 30 minutes.
Serves: 4

CHICKEN PATTIES

The softness of the chicken patties and the creaminess of the sauce make this dish a perfect match for mashed potatoes.

¾ cup dry bread crumbs, herb seasoned
½ cup hot water
1 (10¾-ounce) can cream of chicken soup, divided
2 eggs, lightly beaten
2 (5-ounce) cans chicken, broken into small pieces
1 tablespoon butter
½ soup can milk

1. In a small bowl, mix bread crumbs with water; set aside to soften.

2. In a medium bowl, combine half of the soup with the eggs; mix well.

3. Add moistened bread crumbs and chicken to egg mixture; mix well. Form into patties.

4. In a large skillet, melt butter over low heat, tilt pan to coat entire bottom.

5. Place patties side by side into skillet; cook over low heat, turning over after lightly browned to brown other side.

6. Meanwhile, in a small saucepan heat remaining soup and milk; stir and cook until smooth and heated throughout. Spoon sauce over chicken patties to serve.

Serves: 4 – 6

CHICKEN STEW-GHETTI

So easy to make, so enjoyable to eat!

1 tablespoon olive oil
2 cloves garlic, chopped
1 medium onion, finely chopped
1 small green pepper, finely chopped
1 (15½-ounce) jar pasta sauce
2 cups cooked chicken, finely chopped
1 cup mushrooms, sliced
1 small zucchini, peeled and thinly sliced
¾ cup water
1 teaspoon basil
½ pound spaghetti, uncooked
¼ cup Parmesan cheese (optional)

1. In a large skillet, heat olive oil; add garlic, onion, and green pepper; stir and cook until softened, about 5 minutes.
2. Add pasta sauce, chicken, mushrooms, zucchini, water and basil; stir.
3. Cover; cook over low heat for 30-45 minutes, or until vegetables are tender.
4. Meanwhile, cook spaghetti according to package directions; drain.
5. Serve stew over hot spaghetti noodles; sprinkle with cheese if desired.
Serves: 4 – 6

CHILI MAC

This is the dish for chili lovers. Add more chili powder for an even spicier dish. This recipe uses softer beans in place of the traditional, yet chewier, kidney beans.

1 pound lean ground beef
1 cup onion, finely chopped
½ cup green pepper, finely chopped
1 (15-ounce) can diced tomatoes, undrained
1 (8-ounce) can tomato sauce
½ (6-ounce) can tomato paste
1 tablespoon chili powder
1 teaspoon garlic powder
1 teaspoon salt
¼ teaspoon black pepper
1 (15½-ounce) can pinto or great northern beans
1 cup elbow macaroni, uncooked
½ cup Monterey Jack cheese, shredded

1. In a large skillet, cook beef, onion, and green pepper; break beef apart with spoon as it cooks, until it becomes browned and crumbly. Drain fat.
2. Add the undrained tomatoes, tomato sauce, tomato paste, chili powder, garlic powder, salt, pepper and beans; mix well, cover and cook over low heat until vegetables are soft, about 15-20 minutes.
3. Meanwhile, cook macaroni according to package instructions; drain.

4. Stir macaroni into meat mixture; cover, continue cooking over low heat 5 minutes, or until heated throughout.

5. Uncover; sprinkle with cheese. Serve.

Serves: 4 – 6

CREAMY BEEF OVER MASHED POTATOES

Using purchased mashed potatoes makes for a quick and simple meal. You could also use biscuits or noodles instead of potatoes, if preferred. For a thinner sauce, just add more water or some milk.

1 (24-ounce) package refrigerated mashed potatoes
1 pound lean ground beef
½ cup onions, finely chopped
1 (10¾-ounce) can cream of mushroom soup
½ cup sour cream
¼ cup water
¼ teaspoon black pepper

1. In a large skillet, cook beef and onion; breaking beef apart with spoon as it cooks, until it becomes browned and crumbly. Drain fat.
2. Add soup, sour cream, water, and pepper; stir to blend.
3. Cook over low heat until heated throughout.
4. Meanwhile, heat mashed potatoes according to package directions.
5. Spoon mashed potatoes onto individual serving dishes; top with beef sauce to serve.
Serves: 4 – 6

FISH CAKES

You can make these pan fried patty cakes as thin or thick as you like.

½ cup water
1 pound white fish
2 eggs, lightly beaten
1 teaspoon onion powder
2 tablespoons Dijon mustard
½ teaspoon lemon powder
⅛ teaspoon cayenne pepper
1 cup fresh bread crumbs
¼ cup vegetable oil

1. In a medium skillet, heat water; add fish and simmer until opaque and flakes easily.
2. Remove cooked fish with a slotted spoon to drain; place in a medium bowl and break fish apart into small pieces.
3. In a separate bowl, combine eggs, onion, mustard, lemon, cayenne pepper, and bread crumbs. Let sit a couple minutes to ensure bread crumbs are softened.
4. Add fish to bread crumb mixture; mix well.
5. Form fish mixture into cakes, or patties, at least an inch thick.
6. Heat oil in a large skillet; place fish cakes side by side in skillet and cook over medium heat until lightly browned; flip over and brown on other side.
Yield: 6

FRANKS AND BEANS

This simple time-honored dish is a quick and tasty treat on a busy day. It can be eaten by itself or over toast, and also goes well with corn bread as a side.

2 teaspoons vegetable oil
¼ cup onion, finely chopped
1 (16-ounce) can pork and beans in tomato sauce
1 tablespoon catsup
5 frankfurters, cut into 1-inch slices
6 slices soft bread, lightly toasted (optional)

1. In a medium saucepan, heat oil over medium heat; add onion and cook until tender.

2. Add pork and beans and catsup to saucepan; mix well.

3. Cook uncovered for 10-15 minutes, or until bubbly.

4. Stir in frankfurter slices; cook until heated throughout.

5. Serve over toast if desired.

Serves: 6

IRISH STEW

A delicious one-dish meal. The beef turns out nice and tender, however, it depends on your chewing strength if even tender stew beef cubes are soft enough for you. As with any meat, the quality of the meat plus length of time cooking add to the tenderness.

1½ tablespoons butter
1½ pounds stew beef, cubed
1 (10¾-ounce) can classic tomato soup
¼ soup can water
6 carrots, peeled and quartered
4 large potatoes, peeled and quartered
2 medium onions, peeled and quartered
1 teaspoon salt
½ teaspoon black pepper
2 teaspoons parsley flakes
2 bay leaves

1. In a large skillet, melt butter; add the beef and brown over medium heat. When browned, add soup and water; stir.
2. Add carrots, potatoes, onions, salt, pepper, parsley, and bay leaves.
3. Cover; cook over low heat for 5 hours, or until beef and vegetables are very tender; stir occasionally. Remove bay leaves before serving.
Serves: 6

ITALIAN SUPPER IN A SKILLET

This tasty dish is quick to throw together. Be sure to slice the squash very thin as the thinner you slice it the softer it will be.

½ pound lean ground beef
1 small green pepper, finely chopped
1 small onion, finely chopped
1 clove garlic, finely chopped
1 (15½–ounce) jar pasta sauce with mushrooms
1½ cups hot water
4 ounces egg noodles, uncooked
1 small yellow squash, peeled, halved and thinly sliced
salt and pepper to taste
½ cup Mozzarella cheese, shredded

1. In a large skillet, cook beef, onion, green pepper, and garlic; break beef apart with spoon as it cooks, until it becomes browned and crumbly. Drain fat.
2. Add pasta sauce, hot water, uncooked noodles, squash, salt and pepper, mixing well. Cover; cook over low heat until all ingredients are tender, about 25 minutes.
3. Uncover; continue cooking until mixture is of desired thickness; stir often.
4. Sprinkle with Mozzarella cheese before serving; cover and let stand until cheese melts, about 3 minutes.
Serves: 4

MINI-MEATLOAVES ITALIANO

I really like the convenience of making individual meatloaves on the stovetop instead of one large meatloaf in the oven. Each person gets their own little meatloaf, served right from the stovetop.

1 egg, lightly beaten
1 cup herb seasoned stuffing mix
¼ cup onion, finely chopped
¼ cup green pepper, finely chopped
¼ cup milk
2 tablespoons Parmesan cheese
2 tablespoons parsley flakes
¼ teaspoon salt
¼ teaspoon black pepper
1 cup pasta sauce, divided
1 pound ground beef

1. In a medium bowl, add egg, stuffing mix, onion, green pepper, milk, Parmesan cheese, parsley, salt, black pepper, and 1 tablespoon pasta sauce; combine well.

2. Add ground beef to egg mixture; mix well.

3. Using ½ cup beef mixture at a time, shape into small meatloaves.

4. In a large skillet, place ¼ cup pasta sauce evenly around bottom of skillet; put mini-meatloaves side by side on top of pasta sauce in skillet; spoon 2 tablespoons pasta sauce on top of each mini-meatloaf.

5. Cover; cook over medium heat for 30 minutes, or until cooked throughout.

Serves: 6

SAUCY BEEF AND CABBAGE

There is nothing fancy about this dish, but its simplicity makes it a good, and good-tasting, quick meal.

1 pound lean ground beef
1 medium onion, finely chopped
1 teaspoon garlic powder
2 teaspoons seasoned salt
¼ teaspoon black pepper
1 (10¾-ounce) can cream of onion soup
¼ cup water
3 cups green cabbage, shredded or finely chopped
1 (8-ounce) package egg noodles
½ soup can milk

1. In a large skillet, cook ground beef and onion, stirring until ground beef is browned and crumbly and onions are softened. Drain fat.

2. Add garlic powder, seasoned salt, pepper, and soup; mix well.

3. Stir in water and cabbage; cover and cook over low heat 25 minutes, or until cabbage is tender.

4. Meanwhile, cook noodles according to package directions; drain.

5. Stir noodles and milk into beef mixture.

6. Cover; simmer for 5 minutes, or until heated throughout. Serve.

Serves: 6

SIMPLY SOFT CHICKEN

This simple dish is one my family always finds satisfying. You can add peas or another favorite vegetable into the sauce while cooking. You will want to cook the vegetable before adding to be sure it is soft enough.

1 (13-ounce) can chicken
1 (10¾-ounce) can cream of onion soup
¼ soup can milk
¼ teaspoon black pepper
1 (24-ounce) package refrigerated mashed potatoes

1. In a medium bowl, break chicken apart into small pieces, removing any gristle or bone.
2. In a medium saucepan, add chicken, soup, milk, and pepper. Stir and cook over low heat until soup becomes creamy and mixture is hot.
3. Meanwhile, heat mashed potatoes according to package directions.
4. Spoon mashed potatoes onto individual serving dishes; top with chicken mixture.
Serves: 4

SKILLET CHICKEN WITH BROCCOLI

When I'm in a hurry, I substitute an 8-ounce can of green beans for the broccoli – it saves the steps of cooking and chopping the broccoli that are needed to soften the broccoli.

1 (8-ounce) package linguine noodles
1 tablespoon butter
1 cup broccoli florets, cooked and finely chopped
2 cups chicken, finely chopped
1 (10¾-ounce) can cream of mushroom soup
¾ soup can milk
½ cup Parmesan cheese, grated
¼ teaspoon black pepper

1. Cook noodles according to package directions; drain.

2. Transfer noodles to a large skillet; add butter and stir until noodles are coated and butter is melted.

3. Add broccoli, chicken, soup, milk, cheese, and pepper; mix well.

4. Cover; cook over low heat until mixture is hot and bubbly, about 15–20 minutes, stirring often.

Serves: 4

SPAGHETTI CARBONARA

This is a tasty dish. I make it as a main dish and serve with soft vegetables on the side; however, this also makes a good side dish for anyone who needs to add protein to their diet.

8 ounces spaghetti, uncooked
2 eggs, lightly beaten
3 slices veggie bacon, crisp, crumbled
½ cup Parmesan cheese, grated
2 tablespoons olive oil
¼ teaspoon garlic powder
¼ teaspoon black pepper

1. In a medium saucepan, cook spaghetti according to package instructions; drain.
2. Meanwhile, in a medium bowl, add eggs, bacon, cheese, olive oil, garlic and pepper; whisk together.
3. Cooking over low heat, pour egg mixture over hot spaghetti; toss together until spaghetti is coated and eggs are cooked. Serve.
Serves: 4

SPAGHETTI WITH MEAT SAUCE

You can substitute ground chicken or turkey in this recipe. If you want to leave out the meat altogether, just add more vegetables to the sauce and cook on low heat, covered, until all vegetables are soft.

2 tablespoons olive oil
½ cup onion, finely chopped
2 cloves garlic, finely chopped
⅓ cup carrot, finely grated
½ cup green pepper, finely chopped
1 pound ground beef
1 (24-ounce) jar pasta sauce
1 (12-ounce) package spaghetti noodles
½ cup Parmesan cheese, grated

1. In a large skillet, heat oil over medium heat; add onion, garlic, carrot, and green pepper; stir and cook until vegetables become softened, about 5 minutes.

2. Add ground beef, breaking apart with spoon as it cooks, until it becomes browned and crumbly. Drain fat.

3. Add pasta sauce; mix well. Cover; cook over low heat for 25 minutes, stirring occasionally.

4. Meanwhile, cook spaghetti according to package directions; drain.

5. Serve meat sauce over cooked spaghetti noodles.

6. Sprinkle with Parmesan cheese.

Serves: 4 – 6

STIR-FRIED RICE

This is a wonderful quick to fix one-dish meal. A perfect dish to make at the end of a busy day. Keeping cooked rice in the freezer to have on hand makes this dish quicker yet.

3 tablespoons peanut or vegetable oil, divided
2 cloves garlic, finely chopped
1 green onion, thinly sliced
1 (8-ounce) can mixed peas and carrots, drained
3 eggs, lightly beaten
2 cups long-grain white rice, cooked
2½ tablespoons chicken broth
2½ tablespoons soy sauce

1. In a medium skillet, heat 2 tablespoons of oil over high heat. Add garlic and onions, stirring constantly for 30 seconds.
2. Add the peas and carrots; stir until heated throughout and transfer vegetables to a bowl.
3. Heat 1 tablespoon of oil in the skillet; add the beaten eggs and scramble until almost firm.
4. Add rice to skillet and stir until egg and rice are well blended.
5. Add broth, soy sauce and vegetables; stir fry for 2-3 minutes. Serve.
Serves: 2 – 4

Tortellini with Italian-style Vegetables

There are many different kinds of tortellini, and any of your favorites will go well in this recipe.

¼ cup olive oil
1 cup onion, finely chopped
2 cloves garlic, finely chopped
3 cups fresh spinach leaves, stems removed, finely chopped
1 cup tomatoes, peeled, diced
2 tablespoons water
1 (9-ounce) package refrigerated tortellini

1. In a large skillet, heat oil over medium heat; add onion and garlic. Cook and stir until softened, about 5 minutes.
2. Add spinach; gently stir until leaves begin to wilt.
3. Add tomatoes and water; stir. Cover; cook over low heat 10–15 minutes, until vegetables are tender.
4. Meanwhile, cook tortellini according to package directions; drain.
5. Transfer tortellini to skillet; stir to combine with vegetables.
Serves: 4

TURKEY Á LA KING

Although usually eaten over baking powder biscuits, if you aren't a biscuit fan, this wonderful turkey sauce can be eaten over rice, mashed potatoes, or even pastry puffs. No turkey on hand? Use chicken or tuna instead.

2 tablespoons butter
¾ cup fresh mushrooms, sliced or finely chopped
1 tablespoon flour
1 cup chicken broth
½ cup half-and-half
1½ cups cooked turkey, finely chopped
½ cup peas, cooked
½ teaspoon pimento, finely chopped
½ teaspoon salt
¼ teaspoon black pepper
4 soft baking powder biscuits, halved

1. In a medium skillet, melt butter over medium heat; add mushrooms and cook until tender.
2. Add flour; stir until smooth. Add chicken broth and whisk until slightly thickened.
3. Stir in half-and-half, turkey, peas, pimento, salt and pepper.
4. Cook over low heat until sauce is thickened to desired consistency.
5. To serve, spoon turkey mixture over open biscuits.
Serves: 4

VEGETABLE PRIMAVERA

This is the perfect dish for vegetable lovers. Mix and match your favorite combinations of vegetables. Be sure to choose vegetables that will be soft when cooked, with no hard seeds or skins that might be troublesome.

2 tablespoons olive oil
1 clove garlic, finely chopped
1 cup onions, finely chopped
1 (24-ounce) jar pasta sauce
1 cup broccoli florets, finely chopped
1 cup cauliflower, chopped
1 cup carrots, thinly sliced or shredded
6 ounces spaghetti, uncooked
Parmesan cheese (optional)

1. In a large skillet, heat olive oil; add garlic and onions, cook over medium heat until softened, about 5 minutes.

2. Stir in pasta sauce, broccoli, cauliflower, and carrots.

3. Cover; cook over low heat until vegetables are tender, about 30 minutes.

4. Meanwhile, cook spaghetti noodles according to package directions; drain.

5. Serve vegetable mixture over spaghetti noodles.

6. Sprinkle with Parmesan cheese if desired.

Serves: 6

WELSH RAREBIT

This recipe is a real Welsh treat. Simple and flavorful, it makes for a great light lunch.

1 tablespoon butter
1 cup Cheddar cheese, shredded
2 teaspoons Worcestershire sauce
1 teaspoon dry mustard
2 teaspoons flour
pepper to taste
4 tablespoons beer, flat, at room temperature, or milk
2 slices of soft bread, lightly toasted
1 tomato, peeled and sliced (optional)

1. In a small saucepan, melt butter; add cheese, Worcestershire sauce, mustard, flour, and pepper mix well.
2. Add beer, or milk, to moisten the melting ingredients; stir until smooth.
3. Serve over toast slices.
4. Top with tomato slices if desired.
Serves: 2

ZUCCHINI PATTIES

These patties are very moist, and can be eaten as a light meal by themselves. Try them with a dollop of sour cream or warm applesauce on top.

3 cups zucchini, peeled and shredded
1 teaspoon onion powder
3 eggs, lightly beaten
¾ cup all-purpose or light baking flour
¾ teaspoon baking powder
½ teaspoon salt
¼ teaspoon black pepper
½ teaspoon oregano
2 tablespoons Parmesan cheese, grated (optional)
2 teaspoons vegetable oil

1. Squeeze shredded zucchini to remove excess moisture.

2. In a medium bowl, place zucchini, onion powder, eggs, flour, baking powder, salt, pepper, and oregano, plus Parmesan cheese if desired; mix well.

3. In a large skillet, heat vegetable oil over medium heat.

4. Form zucchini mixture into patties; place side by side in skillet.

5. Cook on one side until lightly browned, turn over and brown other side.

Serves: 6

OVEN

BAKED FISH PARMESAN

This recipe is very simple to make, incredibly soft and tender, and full of flavor.

4 (4-ounce) fish fillets
2 tablespoons butter, melted
1 teaspoon onion powder
salt and pepper to taste
1 (8-ounce) can tomato sauce
½ cup Parmesan cheese

Heat oven to 425 degrees

1. Place fish fillets in a greased shallow baking dish; drizzle ½ tablespoon butter over each fillet, sprinkle each with ¼ teaspoon onion powder, salt and pepper.
2. Spoon ¼ cup tomato sauce over each fillet, sprinkle with Parmesan cheese.
3. Bake in a 425 degree oven for 20 minutes, or until fish is opaque and flakes easily.
Serves: 4

BAKED FISH WITH DILL SAUCE

Fish is a wonderfully light and flakey dish for anyone needing soft food.

4 (4-ounce) fish fillets
2 tablespoons butter, melted
salt and pepper to taste

Dill Sauce
2 tablespoons butter
2 tablespoons flour
½ teaspoon dill
¼ teaspoon salt
⅛ teaspoon white or black pepper
1 cup milk

Heat oven to 350 degrees

1. Place fish in a greased shallow baking dish.
2. Drizzle ½ tablespoon butter over each fillet; sprinkle salt and pepper over each.
3. Bake in a 350 degree oven for 20 minutes, or until fish is opaque in center and flakes easily.
4. Meanwhile, in a small saucepan melt butter; stir in flour, dill, salt and pepper, blending until smooth.
5. Add milk, stirring until near boiling and thickened to desired consistency.
6. Pour dill sauce over baked fish. Serve.
Serves: 4

BEEF AND RICE CASSEROLE

You can use either white or brown rice in this dish, just keep in mind that brown rice is chewier than white rice so will not be the best choice for everyone.

1 pound lean ground beef
1 cup onion, finely chopped
3 cloves garlic, finely chopped
½ cup green pepper, finely chopped
1 (15-ounce) can tomato sauce
⅔ cup beef broth
1 tablespoon oregano
2 teaspoons Worcestershire sauce
1 tablespoon dried celery flakes
3 cups white or brown rice, cooked

Heat oven to 350 degrees

1. In a large skillet, cook beef, onion, garlic and green pepper; break beef apart with spoon as it cooks, until it becomes browned. Drain fat.
2. Add the tomato sauce, broth, oregano, Worcestershire sauce and celery; stir and cook for an additional 5 minutes.
3. Stir in the cooked rice; mix all ingredients well and pour into a greased 3-quart baking dish.
4. Cover; bake in a 350 degree oven for 30 minutes, or until bubbly.
Serves: 6 - 8

BEEFY SAUERKRAUT CASSEROLE

Full of flavor, it goes great with mashed potatoes as a side dish. Be sure to finely chop the sauerkraut for easier chewing.

½ cup white rice, uncooked
1 pound lean ground beef
1 (8-ounce) package mushrooms, sliced or chopped
1 onion, finely chopped
2 cloves garlic, finely chopped
1 teaspoon Worcestershire sauce
½ teaspoon black pepper
1 (8-ounce) can tomato sauce
½ cup sour cream
2 cups sauerkraut, drained
1 cup fresh bread crumbs
1 tablespoon butter, melted

Heat oven to 350 degrees

1. Cook rice according to package directions; drain.
2. In a large skillet, cook beef, mushrooms, onion, and garlic; break beef apart with spoon as it cooks, until it becomes browned and crumbly. Drain fat.
3. Stir in cooked rice, Worcestershire sauce, pepper, tomato sauce, and sour cream.
4. Place one third of the sauerkraut on the bottom of a 2-quart baking dish; top the sauerkraut with half the meat mixture; place another third of the sauerkraut in the baking dish on top of the meat, then the remaining half of

the meat mixture on top of the sauerkraut. Place the remaining sauerkraut on top of the meat mixture.

5. In a small bowl, mix bread crumbs and melted butter together. Sprinkle evenly on top of sauerkraut casserole.

6. Cover; bake in a 350 degree oven for 35 minutes, or until bubbly.

Serves: 4 - 6

CHEESE AND SPINACH SOUFFLÉ

Perfect for the times when you only want a light meal. So light and fluffy, yet packed with protein. Have a soft salad on the side and enjoy!

⅓ cup cooked spinach, finely chopped
3 tablespoons butter
3 tablespoons all-purpose flour
½ teaspoon salt
½ teaspoon tarragon
⅛ teaspoon nutmeg
1 cup milk
1 cup Swiss cheese, shredded
6 eggs, separated

Heat oven to 375 degrees

1. Squeeze cooled spinach to remove excess moisture; set aside.
2. In a medium saucepan, melt 3 tablespoons butter over medium heat; stir in flour, salt, tarragon, and nutmeg. Stir and cook until smooth and bubbly.
3. Slowly pour in milk, stirring constantly until mixture thickens; add cheese, stirring until cheese melts.
4. Remove from heat; whisk in egg yolks, one at a time, until well blended.
5. Stir in spinach; set mixture aside.
6. In a medium bowl, beat egg whites until soft peaks form. Gently fold half of egg whites into cheese mixture, then gently fold in remaining egg whites.

7. Pour into a greased 2-quart soufflé dish or deep baking dish; bake in a 375 degree oven for 25 minutes, or until lightly browned and firm.

Serves: 4

CHEESEBURGER PIE

This is a soft version of the much loved cheeseburger, with all the same wonderful flavors. This is a big hit even with those who don't need their foods to be soft.

1 pound lean ground beef
1 cup onion, finely chopped
1½ cups milk
3 eggs
¾ cup baking mix
½ teaspoon salt
¼ teaspoon black pepper
4 slices American cheese, cut in half
2 tomatoes, peeled and sliced (optional)

Heat oven to 375 degrees

1. In a medium skillet, cook ground beef and onion, stirring until ground beef is browned and crumbly and onions are softened. Drain fat.

2. Grease a 10-inch pie plate; spread ground beef mixture in bottom of pie plate.

3. In a medium bowl, whisk together milk, eggs, baking mix, salt and pepper until smooth.

4. Pour egg mixture over the ground beef.

5. Bake in a 375 degree oven for 30 minutes, or until knife inserted in center comes out clean.

6. Place cheese around top of cheeseburger pie; top with fresh tomato slices if desired.

Serves: 6

CHICKEN CASSEROLE

This simple yet versatile dish can be served over noodles, mashed potatoes, or eaten with your favorite soft side dish.

4 cups cooked chicken, finely chopped
1 (10¾-ounce) can cream of chicken soup
½ cup sour cream
½ teaspoon celery seed
1 (8-ounce) can diced carrots
½ cup butter flavored crackers, crushed

Heat oven to 350 degrees

1. In a medium bowl, combine chicken, soup, sour cream, celery seed, carrots, and crackers.

2. Pour into a greased 8x8-inch baking dish.

3. Cover; bake in a 350 degree oven for 30 minutes, or until hot and bubbly.

Serves: 6

CORNBREAD CASSEROLE

A very simple dish to make – I love simple, don't you? You can use one pound of cooked ground beef in place of the chicken in this recipe if you prefer a beef dish.

2 cups chicken, finely chopped
1 (8-ounce) can sliced carrots, drained
1 (10¾-ounce) can cream of mushroom soup
½ cup milk
1 (8½-ounce) box corn muffin mix
2 heaping tablespoons applesauce

Heat oven to 400 degrees

1. Spread chicken evenly around bottom of greased 8x8-inch baking dish; place carrots over chicken.
2. In a small bowl, combine soup and milk; pour over chicken and carrots.
3. Make corn muffin mix according to package directions, stir in the applesauce.
4. Spoon corn muffin mix onto chicken casserole; bake in a 400 degree oven for 20 minutes, or until muffin mix is lightly browned.
Serves: 4

ITALIAN STYLE BEEF CASSEROLE

Whether Italian dishes are a favorite of yours or not, you'll like this easy pasta meal.

1 pound ground beef
¼ cup onion, finely chopped
¼ cup green pepper, finely chopped
1 garlic clove, chopped
1 (6-ounce) can tomato paste
½ cup water
½ teaspoon oregano
¼ cup parsley flakes
1 teaspoon salt
1 (8-ounce) package noodles
½ cup parmesan cheese, grated
2 eggs, lightly beaten
½ cup mayonnaise
½ cup Mozzarella cheese, shredded (optional)

Heat oven to 350 degrees

1. In a large skillet, add beef, onion, green pepper and garlic; break beef apart with spoon as it cooks, until it becomes browned and crumbly. Drain fat.

2. Stir in tomato paste, water, oregano, parsley and salt; cover and simmer for 10 minutes.

3. Meanwhile, cook noodles according to package instructions; drain.

4. In a medium bowl, combine the Parmesan cheese, eggs, and mayonnaise.

5. Put half of the cooked noodles in a 6x10-inch greased baking dish, spread half of the egg mixture over the noodles, then half of the meat sauce; place the remaining noodles, egg mixture, and meat sauce into baking dish in the same order, with meat sauce on top.

6. Cover; bake in a 350 degree oven for 30 minutes, or until bubbly.

7. Sprinkle with shredded Mozzarella cheese if desired. Serve.

Serves: 6

JOHNNY MARZETTI

This is a dish that I remember from my childhood. It's been around for years, and for good reason!

1 pound ground chuck
1½ tablespoons dried celery flakes
1 large onion, finely chopped
1 bell pepper, finely chopped
1 clove garlic, finely chopped
1 (15-ounce) can tomato sauce
½ teaspoon salt
½ teaspoon black pepper
½ teaspoon paprika
1 teaspoon Worcestershire sauce
1 (10-ounce) package Kluski noodles
1½ cups Mozzarella cheese
¼ cup Parmesan cheese, grated
¼ cup black olives, chopped

Heat oven to 325 degrees

1. In a medium skillet, cook ground beef, onion, bell pepper, and garlic, stirring until ground beef is browned and crumbly and vegetables are softened. Drain fat.
2. Add tomato sauce, tomato paste, salt, pepper, paprika and Worcestershire sauce to meat mixture; mix well.
3. Meanwhile, in a medium saucepan, cook noodles according to package directions; drain.
4. Grease a 2½ quart casserole dish; place half of the cooked noodles in the bottom of the casserole dish, then

103

layer half of the meat mixture over the noodles; sprinkle half the Mozzarella cheese on top of the meat mixture then sprinkle with Parmesan cheese. Repeat layers with noodles, then meat mixture, and remaining Mozzarella cheese on top. Sprinkle chopped olives over top.

5. Cover; bake in a 325 degree oven for 30 minutes, or until bubbly.

Serves: 6 - 8

MACARONI AND CHEESE

Who can go wrong with macaroni and cheese? Use your favorite cheese, and choose any pasta shape or noodle to create a dish to meet your taste.

8 ounces elbow macaroni
3 tablespoons butter
2 eggs, lightly beaten
1 (12-ounce) can evaporated milk
1 teaspoon prepared mustard
¼ teaspoon black pepper
1 teaspoon Worcestershire sauce
2½ cups cheddar cheese

Heat oven to 350 degrees

1. In a medium saucepan, cook macaroni according to package instructions; drain, add butter to macaroni in saucepan, stirring to coat macaroni.
2. Meanwhile, in a medium bowl, add eggs, 1 cup milk, mustard, pepper and Worcestershire sauce; whisk together.
3. Pour egg mixture and 2 cups cheese over macaroni; cook over low heat, stirring gently until well combined and cheese melts; gradually stir in remaining cheese and enough milk until consistency is creamy.
4. Pour into a 1½-quart baking dish; cover, and bake at 350 degrees for 25 minutes.
Serves: 4

MANICOTTI

This dish can be made with or without meat. Simply add a half pound of cooked ground beef to the pasta sauce if meat is desired.

14 manicotti shells, uncooked
2 tablespoons olive oil
1 clove garlic, finely chopped
1 cup mushrooms, finely chopped
2 cups Ricotta cheese
⅔ cup Parmesan cheese, grated, divided
¼ teaspoon black pepper
1 (26-ounce) jar pasta sauce with garlic and onions

Heat oven to 350 degrees

1. Cook manicotti shells according to package instructions; set aside to cool.
2. Heat oil in a skillet; add garlic and mushrooms; cook and stir until softened, about 5 minutes.
3. In a medium bowl, mix Ricotta cheese, ⅓ cup Parmesan cheese, mushrooms, garlic and pepper.
4. Spread ⅓ of the pasta sauce around the bottom of a 9x13-inch baking dish.
5. Fill manicotti shells with Ricotta mixture; place shells side by side on top of sauce in baking dish.
6. Pour remaining pasta sauce evenly over the top of the shells; sprinkle with the remaining Parmesan cheese.
7. Cover; bake in a 350 degree oven for 30 minutes, or until bubbly.
Serves: 7

MEAT LOAF

You will love this version of the classic meat loaf recipe. It is both moist and flavorful. The bacon on top gives extra flavor but can be left off or removed after baking.

1 tablespoon vegetable oil
1 medium onion, finely chopped
2 cloves garlic, finely chopped
1½ pounds ground chuck
½ pound ground pork
2 eggs, lightly beaten
1 teaspoon thyme
1 teaspoon salt
½ teaspoon black pepper
2 teaspoons Dijon mustard

2 teaspoons Worcestershire sauce
½ cup buttermilk or plain yogurt
1⅓ cup fresh bread crumbs
2 tablespoons parsley
6 slices thin-sliced bacon

Glaze
¼ cup ketchup
2 tablespoons brown sugar
2 teaspoons vinegar

Heat oven to 350 degrees

1. In a small skillet, add vegetable oil; cook onion and garlic over low heat until softened. Set aside to cool.

2. In a large bowl, place ground chuck and pork; add eggs, thyme, salt, pepper, mustard, Worcestershire sauce, buttermilk or yogurt, bread crumbs, parsley, and cooked onion and garlic; mix well.

3. Form meat mixture into a loaf shape and place on a wire rack that is covered with aluminum foil; make several holes in the foil for the fat to drip through. Place the rack into a shallow baking dish.

4. In a small bowl, mix the ketchup, brown sugar, and vinegar; spread all over the meat loaf.

5. Place the bacon slices in a criss-cross pattern across the top of the meat loaf, tucking the ends under the meat loaf, as needed.

6. Bake in a 350 degree oven for 1 hour, or until loaf is cooked through.

Serves: 6 - 8

SHEPHERD'S PIE

Shepherd's Pie has been around for many years, and there are several versions. Some recipes call for a tomato based sauce, some gravy for sauce, while this recipe has a creamy style sauce.

1 pound ground beef
½ cup onion, finely chopped
½ cup green beans, cooked
½ cup carrot slices, cooked
1 (10¾-ounce) can cream of mushroom soup
½ soup can milk
½ teaspoon basil
salt and pepper to taste
4 cups mashed potatoes
½ cup Cheddar cheese, shredded

Heat oven to 350 degrees

1. In a medium skillet, cook ground beef and onion; stir until ground beef is browned and crumbly and onion is softened. Drain fat.

2. Add green beans, carrots, soup, milk, basil, salt and pepper; stir to mix.

3. Place meat mixture in a greased 2½ quart casserole dish.

4. Spoon mashed potatoes evenly over meat mixture.

5. Cover; bake in a 350 degree oven for 25 minutes, or until bubbly.

6. Remove from oven, top with Cheddar cheese; return to oven for 5 minutes, or until cheese is melted.

Serves: 4 - 6

109

SPAGHETTI PIE

This is a fun and tasty main dish pie. You can use two cups of your favorite pasta sauce in place of the tomato sauce and spices if you prefer. And be sure to use a deep dish baking dish so it won't overflow!

1 pound ground beef
⅓ cup onion, finely chopped
¼ cup green pepper, finely chopped
1 (8-ounce) can tomato sauce
1 (6-ounce) tomato paste
1 teaspoon sugar
1 teaspoon oregano
½ teaspoon basil
1 teaspoon garlic powder
½ cup mozzarella cheese
6 ounces spaghetti noodles, uncooked
2 tablespoons butter
⅓ cup Parmesan cheese
2 eggs, lightly beaten
1 cup ricotta cheese

Heat oven to 350 degrees

1. In a medium skillet, cook ground beef, onion, and green pepper; stir until ground beef is browned and crumbly and vegetables are softened. Drain fat.
2. Add tomato sauce, tomato paste, sugar, oregano, basil and garlic powder. Stir to combine, cover and cook over low heat for 25 minutes.

3. Meanwhile, cook spaghetti according to package directions; drain.

4. Add butter, Parmesan cheese, and eggs to hot spaghetti; mix well.

5. Place spaghetti mixture into a deep-dish 10-inch pie dish, forming a "crust"; add the ricotta cheese, spreading it over the top of the spaghetti crust.

6. Pour meat mixture into the pie dish.

7. Cover; bake in a 350 degree oven for 25 minutes; remove from oven, top with mozzarella cheese and return to oven for 5 minutes, or until cheese is melted.

Serves: 6

TUNA NOODLE CASSEROLE

Who says "No" to this family favorite? It's so easy to make, and filling too. Just add your favorite vegetable, or leave out the vegetables altogether.

1 (8-ounce) package egg noodles
1 (10¾-ounce) can cream of mushroom soup
1 soup can milk
2 teaspoons onion powder
2 teaspoons dried celery flakes
½ teaspoon black pepper
2 (6-ounce) cans tuna, drained
1 (8-ounce) can peas, drained

Heat oven to 350 degrees

1. In a medium saucepan, cook noodles according to package directions; drain.
2. Meanwhile, in a large bowl, combine soup, milk, onion powder, celery flakes and pepper; stir until smooth. Add tuna and peas; mix well.
3. Fold cooked noodles into tuna mixture; pour into greased 3-quart baking dish.
4. Cover; bake in a 350 degree oven for 30 minutes, or until bubbly.
Serves: 6 - 8

TURKEY PUFFS

This is a luscious light meal that helps get rid of those Thanksgiving leftovers.

1 cup heavy cream
3 eggs
1 teaspoon thyme
½ teaspoon salt
¼ teaspoon black pepper
½ cup all-purpose flour
1 cup cooked turkey, finely chopped
½ cup stuffing, precooked and cooled
½ cup Cheddar cheese, shredded

Heat oven to 375 degrees

1. Pour the cream into a blender and whip until it begins to thicken, about 25 seconds.
2. Add the eggs, one at a time, pulse the blender after each addition. Add thyme, salt, pepper, and flour, blending on low until smooth.
3. Grease a 12 cup muffin tin; divide the batter between the muffin cups. Divide the turkey evenly among the cups, dropping the turkey onto the batter.
4. Top each with an equal amount of stuffing; sprinkle with Cheddar cheese.
5. Bake in a 375 degree oven for 20 minutes, or until puffed and lightly browned.
Serves: 6

TURKEY STEW 'N BISCUITS

Whether you are using leftover turkey or turkey from a can, this simple hot-out-of-the-oven dish is a tasty and satisfying meal.

1 tablespoon butter
1 cup frozen diced potatoes, thawed
1 (10-ounce) package frozen mixed vegetables, thawed
¼ cup onion, finely chopped
½ cup water, divided
1 (10-ounce) jar turkey or chicken gravy
2 cups cooked turkey, finely chopped
¼ teaspoon black pepper
¼ teaspoon marjoram
1 tube refrigerated biscuits, flakey style, unbaked

Heat oven to 400 degrees

1. In a large ovenproof skillet, melt the butter over medium heat; add the diced potatoes, mixed vegetables, onion, and ¼ cup water.
2. Cover; cook over low heat until tender, about 20 minutes; add more water if needed to retain moisture.
3. Uncover and stir in gravy, ¼ cup water, turkey, pepper, and marjoram; mix well.
4. Bring to a boil, then remove from heat; arrange biscuits on top of turkey mixture.
5. Bake in a 400 degree oven for 12-14 minutes, or until biscuits are browned.
Serves: 6

SLOWCOOKER

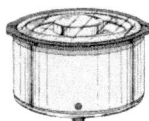

ALMOST LASAGNA

This is a quick and easy lasagna-like dish for the lasagna lovers in the crowd.

1 (8-ounce) package bowtie pasta
1½ pounds lean ground beef
1 medium onion, finely chopped
1 (26-ounce) jar pasta sauce
1½ cups small-curd cottage cheese
1 (16-ounce) package Mozzarella cheese, shredded

1. Cook pasta according to package directions; drain.

2. Meanwhile, in a large skillet, cook ground beef and onion, stirring until ground beef is browned and crumbly and onions are softened. Drain fat.

3. Add pasta sauce to ground beef; stir well.

4. Place half of the ground beef mixture in the bottom of the slow cooker; top with half of the pasta, half of the cottage cheese then half of the Mozzarella cheese.

5. Repeat the layers with the remaining half of the beef, pasta, cottage cheese, then Mozzarella cheese.

6. Cover; cook on Low 5-6 hours.

Serves: 8

APPLE SAUERKRAUT WITH POLISH SAUSAGE

Such a simple yet tasty dish to make, this one goes well with noodles or mashed potatoes. For easier chewing, be sure to finely chop the sauerkraut before adding to slow cooker.

1 (14-ounce) can sauerkraut, finely chopped
1 pound smoked Polish sausage, skinless
2 cooking apples, peeled and sliced
¼ cup brown sugar
½ cup apple cider or apple juice

1. Place half of the sauerkraut in the bottom of a slow cooker.

2. Spread half of the apple slices over the sauerkraut, then sprinkle with half of the brown sugar.

3. Cut the sausage into 1-inch pieces; add to slow cooker.

4. Place the remaining apple slices on top of the sausage, sprinkle apples with remaining brown sugar, then top with the remaining sauerkraut.

5. Pour the apple cider, or juice, over all.

6. Cover; cook on Low for 6 hours.

Serves: 4

BARBEQUE BEEF AND BEANS

Eating this dish with corn bread on the side is a simple yet satisfying meal. This dish uses veggie bacon, because it becomes soft while cooking, however, you can use finely crumbled regular bacon if that is soft enough for you after it cooks in a sauce.

½ pound ground beef
⅓ cup onion, finely chopped
2 slices veggie bacon, crisp, crumbled
1 (15-ounce) can great northern beans
1 (15-ounce) can pinto beans
1 (15-ounce) can pork and beans
½ cup barbeque sauce
¼ cup green pepper, finely chopped (optional)

1. In a medium skillet, cook ground beef and onion, stirring until ground beef is browned and crumbly and onions are softened. Drain fat.

2. In a slow cooker, add all ingredients; mix well.

3. Cover; cook on High heat for 3½ hours, or until onions are of desired softness.

Serves: 8

BEEF PATTY STEW

The addition of red wine gives this stew a depth of flavor you will appreciate.

1 pound ground beef
1 large tomato, peeled and diced
2 carrots, sliced
2 medium onions, sliced
¼ pound fresh mushrooms, sliced
1 tablespoon dried celery flakes
3 medium potatoes, peeled, quartered
1 clove garlic, minced
1 cup beef broth
½ cup red wine
1 teaspoon salt
¼ teaspoon black pepper
3 tablespoons cornstarch

1. Form beef into four patties; place side by side in a large skillet, brown both sides.

2. Place patties in a slow cooker; top with tomato, carrots, onions, mushrooms, celery flakes and potatoes.

3. In a small bowl, combine garlic, beef broth, wine, salt and pepper; mix well.

4. In a separate bowl, mix cornstarch with a few tablespoons of broth mixture; add cornstarch mixture to the broth mixture, stir to combine.

5. Pour broth mixture into slow cooker over beef and vegetables; cook on Low for 6 hours, or until vegetables are tender.

Serves: 4

BEEFY RIGATONI

This dish has few ingredients, is simple to make, and yet is full of flavor.

1 (12-ounce) package of rigatoni pasta
1½ pounds of lean ground beef
1½ cups onions, finely chopped
1 (20-ounce) jar pasta sauce
3 cups Mozzarella cheese, shredded
1 cup fresh mushrooms, finely chopped

1. Cook rigatoni according to package directions; drain.

2. Meanwhile, in a medium skillet, cook ground beef and onions, stirring until ground beef is browned and crumbly and onions are softened. Drain fat.

3. Place half of the pasta sauce in the bottom of the slow cooker; top with half of the ground beef mixture, half of the rigatoni, half of the cheese, and half of the mushrooms.

4. Layer remaining ingredients in same order as Step **3.**

5. Cover; cook on Low 4–5 hours.

Serves: 8 - 10

Chicken Cacciatore

Chicken Cacciatore is delicious served over hot linguini noodles or spaghetti noodles. For even easier chewing, remove cooked chicken, debone, cut into small pieces, then mix chicken pieces back into slow cooker before serving.

2½ pounds chicken legs and thighs
2 medium onions, finely chopped
2 medium green peppers, chopped
1 bay leaf
2 cloves garlic, sliced
1 (16-ounce) can stewed tomatoes
1 (8-ounce) can tomato sauce
½ teaspoon salt
¼ teaspoon black pepper
½ teaspoon oregano
½ teaspoon basil
¼ cup white wine (optional)

1. Place chicken in bottom of slow cooker.

2. Place onions, green peppers, and bay leaf on top of chicken

3. In a medium bowl, combine garlic, tomatoes, tomato sauce, salt, pepper, oregano and basil, plus wine if desired; mix well.

4. Pour tomato mixture over vegetables and chicken.

5. Cover; cook on Low 6–7 hours, or until tender. Remove bay leaf before serving.

6. If needed, remove cooked chicken, debone, and cut into small pieces; mix chicken pieces back into slow cooker.

Serves: 6

CHICKEN STEW

This stew comes out just right – the sauce is not too thick, not too thin. If you prefer dark meat, simply substitute chicken thighs for the breasts.

1½ cups water
1 cup chicken broth
2 (.87- ounce) packages chicken gravy mix
2 cloves garlic, finely chopped
1 tablespoon parsley
½ teaspoon black pepper
5 carrots, peeled, cut into 1 inch slices
1½ cups green beans, frozen or fresh
4 boneless chicken breasts (1½ pounds)
3 tablespoon all-purpose flour
⅓ cup water
1 (6.3-ounce) tube refrigerated buttermilk biscuits

1. Combine 1½ cups water, broth, gravy mix, garlic, parsley, and pepper in slow cooker; mix well. Add carrots, green beans, and chicken.
2. Cover, and cook on Low for 7-8 hours, or until tender.
3. Remove cooked chicken and cut into small pieces; set aside.
4. In a small bowl, combine flour and ⅓ cup water; stir into slow cooker.
5. Mix in chicken pieces; cover, set control on High and cook one more hour.
6. Meanwhile, bake biscuits according to package directions; serve chicken stew on top of halved biscuits.
Serves: 4 - 6

CHICKEN TETRAZZINI

If you prefer dark meat, just substitute boneless chicken thighs for the breasts in this recipe.

1¼ pounds chicken breast tenderloins
1 cup chicken broth
½ cup white wine
1 medium onion, finely chopped
¼ teaspoon dried thyme
1 teaspoon salt
½ teaspoon black pepper
2½ tablespoons cornstarch
¼ cup water
1 cup fresh mushrooms, finely chopped
½ cup half-and-half or whole milk
½ pound spaghetti, broken into 3-inch pieces
½ cup Parmesan cheese, grated

1. Add chicken to slow cooker.
2. In a medium bowl, combine broth, wine, onion, thyme, salt and pepper; pour over chicken.
3. Cover; cook on Low for 5 hours, or until chicken is tender; break chicken into bite sized pieces.
4. In a small bowl, combine cornstarch and water; stir until smooth. Add cornstarch mixture to slow cooker; stir, and add mushrooms; cover; cook on High for 20 minutes.
5. Meanwhile, cook spaghetti according to package; drain.
6. Stir half-and-half, spaghetti, and cheese into slow cooker. Cover; cook on High another 5 minutes, or until heated throughout.
Serves: 6

CHICKEN WITH BROCCOLI AND RICE

This dish is quick and easy to make. It can be put together the night before and kept in the refrigerator until ready to cook the next day.

2 tablespoons vegetable oil
1 medium onion, finely chopped
1 clove garlic, finely chopped
2 cups fresh or frozen broccoli florets, chopped
2 cups cooked chicken, finely chopped
1 (10¾-ounce) can cream of chicken soup
1 (12-ounce) can evaporated milk
3 cups white rice, cooked
1½ cups Cheddar cheese, shredded
½ teaspoon black pepper
½ cup fresh mushrooms, finely chopped

1. In a large skillet, heat the oil over medium heat; add the onion, garlic, and broccoli, cooking and stirring until softened, about 5 minutes.

2. In a large bowl, combine broccoli mixture, chicken, soup, evaporated milk, rice, cheese, pepper, and mushrooms; mix well.

3. Pour into slow cooker.

4. Cover; cook on Low for 3 hours.

Serves: 4 - 6

CREAMY CHICKEN AND NOODLES

The chicken comes out so tender. However, if you need extra softness, when the chicken is cooked remove the chicken from the slow cooker and take the meat off the bones. Finely chop the chicken then stir back into the slow cooker.

2 (10¾-ounce) cans cream of chicken soup
1½-2 pounds chicken legs and thighs
2 cups carrots, peeled and sliced
1½ cups onion, chopped
1 cup peas, frozen or fresh
1 bay leaf
1 tablespoon parsley
½ cup water
1 teaspoon thyme
¼ teaspoon black pepper
1 (8-ounce) package noodles

1. Spread one can of soup around bottom of slow cooker; place chicken pieces side by side on top of soup.
2. Place carrots, onions, peas, and bay leaf on top of chicken.
3. In a medium bowl, combine remaining soup, parsley, water, thyme, and pepper; pour into slow cooker over chicken and vegetables.
4. Cover; cook on Low for 8 hours, or until tender.
5. Cook noodles according to package directions; drain.
6. Spoon chicken and vegetables over noodles to serve.
Serves: 4 - 6

CREAMY PORK CHOPS

This is a wonderfully quick and easy dish to put together, and the pork chops come out so tender you can cut them with your fork. For extra softness, remove the cooked pork chops from the slow cooker, take the meat off the bones, finely chop the meat, then stir back into the slow cooker.

6 pork chops
1 (14¾-ounce) can cream of chicken soup
½ teaspoon garlic powder
1½ teaspoons dry mustard

1. Spread half of soup evenly across bottom of slow cooker.

2. Place pork chops side by side on top of soup.

3. In a medium bowl, combine remaining soup, garlic, and mustard. Spread over pork chops.

4. Cover; cook on Low 8-9 hours, or under tender.

Serves: 6

SAUCY CHOPPED STEAKS

So tender and delicious. Any type of chopped steak can be used in this recipe. Serve these soft steaks with your favorite soft side dish.

1 (10¾-ounce) can cream of mushroom soup
4 chopped steaks
1 large onion, chopped
2 carrots, peeled, cut into 1 inch slices

1. Place half of the soup into slow cooker; spread evenly across bottom.
2. Place steaks side-by-side in slow cooker; spoon remaining soup evenly over top of steaks.
3. Place onions and carrots on top.
4. Cook on Low for 8 hours, or until tender.
Serves: 4

SCALLOPED POTATOES AND HAM

This dish should be called "impossible scalloped potatoes" as it has little liquid yet turns out soft and tasty.

2 (6-ounce) cans ground smoked ham
8 medium potatoes, thinly sliced
2 small onions, finely chopped
¼ teaspoon black pepper
1 cup Cheddar cheese, shredded
1 (10¾-ounce) can cream of mushroom soup
⅔ soup can milk

1. In a small bowl, break the ham into small pieces.

2. Place half of the ham, potatoes, and onions into slow cooker; sprinkle the cheese and pepper over the top.

3. Layer the remaining ham, potatoes, and onions into slow cooker.

4. In a medium bowl, combine soup with milk; pour soup mixture into the slow cooker evenly over the top of the potato mixture.

5. Cover; cook on Low for 7-8 hours, or until tender.

Serves: 6 - 8

SLOW COOKER LASAGNA

You may find that the lasagna noodles must be broken to fit the shape of your slow cooker, but it is worth the effort to be able to enjoy this fairly effortless lasagna dish.

1 pound lean ground beef
1 medium onion, finely chopped
2 cloves garlic, sliced
1 (29-ounce) can tomato sauce
1 cup water
1 (6-ounce) can tomato paste
½ teaspoon salt
½ teaspoon basil
1 teaspoon oregano
1 (8-ounce) package lasagna noodles, uncooked
4 cups Mozzarella cheese, shredded
1½ cups small-curd cottage cheese
½ cup Parmesan cheese, grated

1. In a large skillet, cook ground beef, onion, and garlic; stir until beef is browned and crumbly. Drain fat.
2. Add tomato sauce, water, tomato paste, salt, basil, and oregano; mix well.
3. Place one-fourth of meat sauce in bottom of slow cooker.
4. Place one-third of the lasagna noodles evenly on top of the meat in the slow cooker.
5. In a medium bowl, combine Mozzarella cheese, cottage cheese, and Parmesan cheese. Spoon one-third of the

cheese mixture into the slow cooker over the lasagna noodles.

6. Repeat layers with remaining meat, noodles, and cheese, with final layer being meat sauce.

7. Cover; cook on Low for 5 hours, or until tender.

Serves: 6 - 8

Slow Cooker "Pizza"

Use your favorite pizza toppings to make this the right dish for you. The ingredients below are common pizza toppings, but you may like more unusual toppings or simply more toppings!

8 ounces bowtie pasta
1 (16-ounce) jar pizza sauce
½ pound lean ground beef
½ pound bulk sausage
½ pound pepperoni slices, halves or quartered
3 cups Mozzarella cheese, shredded
¼ cup Parmesan cheese, grated
1 cup fresh mushrooms, thinly sliced
½ cup onions, finely chopped
½ cup green pepper, finely chopped
2 cloves garlic, finely chopped

1. Cook pasta according to package directions; drain, place pasta and pizza sauce in slow cooker.

2. Meanwhile, in a large skillet, cook ground beef and sausage, stirring and breaking apart with spoon until they are browned and crumbly. Drain fat.

3. Transfer beef and sausage mixture to slow cooker; add pepperoni, cheese, mushrooms, onions, green pepper, and garlic. Mix well.

4. Cover; cook on Low 4–5 hours.

Serves: 6 - 8

STUFFED CABBAGE ROLLS

Cabbage rolls take a few extra steps to make, but are well worth the effort. They are tender and flavorful, like mini-meatloaves wrapped in cabbage. Be sure to cut the cooked cabbage into small pieces when eating, as large bites could be too chewy.

1 quart water
12 large cabbage leaves, washed
1 pound lean ground beef
1 egg, lightly beaten
½ cup onion, finely chopped
½ cup white or brown rice, cooked
½ teaspoon salt
¼ teaspoon black pepper
½ teaspoon cinnamon
1 (6-ounce) can tomato paste
¾ cup water

1. In a large saucepan, heat water to boiling; remove from heat.
2. Soak cabbage leaves, a few at a time, in the hot water until softened, about 3 - 5 minutes. Drain leaves; set aside to cool.
3. In a large bowl, combine ground beef, egg, onion, rice, salt, pepper, cinnamon, and one tablespoon of tomato paste. Mix well.
4. Lay each cabbage leaf flat, one at a time, and spoon two tablespoons of mixture onto the center; roll up tightly, tucking ends under.

5. Stack stuffed leaves in the bottom of slow cooker.

6. In a small bowl, combine remaining tomato paste with ¾ cup water; pour evenly over the cabbage rolls.

7. Cover; cook on Low 8–9 hours.

Serves: 6

STUFFED GREEN PEPPERS

Pouring most of the sauce into the tops of the stuffed peppers ensures a moist, tender meal. Of course, be sure some of the sauce goes into the bottom of the slow cooker so that the bottoms of the peppers get a nice steam bath!

5 green peppers
1 pound lean ground beef
½ cup onions, finely chopped
½ teaspoon black pepper
1¼ cups white rice, cooked
1 tablespoon Worcestershire sauce
1 (8-ounce) can tomato sauce
¼ cup beef broth

1. Wash green peppers; cut stem ends from peppers; remove seeds and membranes without breaking peppers apart.
2. In a medium skillet, cook ground beef and onion, stirring until ground beef is browned and crumbly and onions are softened. Drain fat.
3. Transfer beef and onions to a large bowl; add pepper, rice, and Worcestershire sauce; mix well.
4. Stuff the green peppers with the meat mixture; stand the stuffed peppers upright in slow cooker.
5. In a small bowl, mix together the tomato sauce and broth; pour evenly over the peppers.
6. Cover; cook on Low for 6 hours or until peppers are tender.
Serves: 5

TAMALE CASSEROLE

A tamale casserole turns out looking like a meat loaf but is spooned out like a casserole. This dish may not be for everyone, as it contains corn, and corn can be difficult to chew for some people.

¾ cup yellow cornmeal
1 cup milk
1 egg, lightly beaten
1 pound lean ground beef
1½ teaspoons chili powder
1 (16-ounce) jar chunky tomato salsa
1 (16-ounce) can whole kernel corn, drained
1 (2¼-ounce) can olives, sliced
1 cup Cheddar or Monterey Jack cheese, shredded

1. In a large bowl, combine cornmeal, milk, and egg, stirring until mixed.
2. Add beef, chili powder, salsa, drained corn, and olives; mix well.
3. Pour mixture into slow cooker.
4. Cover; cook on High 3½-4 hours.
5. Sprinkle cheese over top; serve when cheese begins to melt.
Serves: 6 - 8

COLD SIDE DISHES

Cauliflower Pasta Salad

Tri-color pasta allows this simple pasta salad to make a lovely presentation. If you don't have tri-color pasta available, you can add color to this dish by adding a cup of tender green peas or diced tomatoes.

2 cups cauliflower florets (about 1 small head)
1 (8-ounce) package tri-color rotini or bowtie pasta
¼ cup red onion, finely chopped, or ½ teaspoon onion powder
¼ cup Parmesan cheese, grated
½ cup Italian salad dressing

1. In a medium saucepan, cook the cauliflower in hot water until soft; drain and refrigerate to cool.
2. Meanwhile, in a medium saucepan, cook pasta according to package directions; drain and refrigerate to cool.
3. Cut cauliflower into bite-size pieces, cutting off any tough stalks.
4. In a large bowl, place cooled cauliflower, pasta, onion and Parmesan cheese.
5. Pour salad dressing over cauliflower mixture; toss gently to combine.
6. Cover; refrigerate to chill.
Serves: 8

COOKED CARROT SALAD

This salad is so incredibly simple, and yet so enjoyable. Use any of the various Ranch dressing flavors available, or substitute your favorite salad dressing.

2 cups water
1 tablespoon sugar
1 bunch of carrots
3 tablespoons Ranch dressing

1. Peel carrots and cut each carrot into thirds, crossways.

2. In a medium saucepan, bring water and sugar to a boil; add carrots. Cover; cook over low heat until carrots are soft, about 20-30 minutes.

3. Drain; cover, and refrigerate to chill.

4. Cut cooled carrots into 1-inch pieces and place in a serving dish.

5. Drizzle salad dressing over carrots, serve.

Serves: 4 - 6

CREAMY CUCUMBER SALAD

Sliced very thin, and eaten in small bites, this dish should be soft enough for most cucumber lovers to be able to enjoy the taste of summer. You can also chop cucumber slices into smaller pieces for easier chewing. Refrigerating overnight before serving adds to the softness.

3 medium cucumbers
1 tablespoon sugar
½ cup sour cream
1½ teaspoons salt
½ teaspoon onion powder
1 tablespoon white vinegar

1. Peel cucumbers; cut in half lengthwise, then slice very thin; set aside.
2. In a medium bowl, combine sugar, sour cream, salt, onion powder, and vinegar.
3. Add cucumber slices to bowl; stir until cucumbers are well coated with dressing; refrigerate for several hours to chill and soften.

Serves: 8

GELATIN WITH PEACHES AND COTTAGE CHEESE

Our family has enjoyed this cool side dish for decades. It is especially good on a warm summer day. For an even softer gelatin dish, puree the cottage cheese and peaches before folding them into the gelatin.

1 (.3-ounce) package cherry flavored gelatin
1 cup small curd cottage cheese
1 cup peaches, sliced or diced

1. Prepare gelatin according to package instructions; refrigerate to chill.

2. Meanwhile, cut peach slices into bite sized pieces.

3. When gelatin is almost set, fold in cottage cheese and peaches.

4. Return to refrigerator and chill until firm.

Serves: 4 - 6

HOMEMADE APPLESAUCE

I grew up with mom's homemade applesauce. You will be surprised at how easy it is to make, and how much more flavorful it is than store bought applesauce. Depending on the type of apples you use, you may need a little more or a little less water. Both Cortland and McIntosh apples make a good applesauce.

8 cooking apples
⅓ cup water
⅓ cup sugar
1 teaspoon cinnamon (optional)

1. Peel apples, core, and cut into quarters.

2. Place apples in a medium saucepan; add water.

3. Cover; cook on low heat until apples are very soft and mixture is thickened, about 30 minutes.

4. Mash apple mixture with a potato masher; stir in sugar, and cinnamon if desired, and continue cooking uncovered until applesauce is of desired consistency.

5. Cover; refrigerate to chill.

Serves: 8

LIME-PEAR GELATIN

Smooth and creamy, no one will guess there are healthy ingredients in this tasty side dish.

1 (.3-ounce) package lime gelatin
¾ cup hot water
1 (15-ounce) can pear slices or halves, drained
1 (8-ounce) package cream cheese, softened

1. In a small bowl, dissolve gelatin in hot water.

2. Place gelatin, pears, and cream cheese in a blender; blend until smooth.

3. Pour into an 8x8-inch dish; refrigerate until set.

Serves: 6

MACARONI SALAD

This traditional recipe for macaroni salad is the perfect accompaniment to casual meals or family get-togethers, as it is enjoyed by young and old alike. Don't hesitate to add more hard-cooked eggs if you want to pack in the protein.

1 (8-ounce) package elbow macaroni
4 large eggs, hard-cooked, chopped
½ cup onion, finely chopped, or 1 teaspoon onion powder
¼ cup dill pickle relish
1½ tablespoons sugar
½ teaspoon salt
¼ teaspoon black pepper
½ cup mayonnaise
2 teaspoons prepared mustard

1. Cook the macaroni according to package directions; drain, set aside to cool.
2. In a large bowl, place the cooled macaroni, chopped eggs, and onion.
3. In a small bowl, combine the pickle relish, sugar, salt, pepper, mayonnaise, and mustard; mix well.
4. Pour the pickle relish mixture over the macaroni mixture; stir gently to combine.
5. Cover; refrigerate to chill.
Serves: 8 - 10

MARINATED TOMATO SLICES

A pretty looking dish, this is a simple way to enjoy the fruits of summer. Eat this with bread or rolls, if you like, so you can soak up the tasty sauce.

4 large tomatoes
¼ cup olive oil
1 tablespoon lemon juice
1 teaspoon sugar
½ teaspoon salt
½ teaspoon oregano
1 tablespoon parsley

1. Peel the tomatoes and cut into ½-inch slices; layer in an oblong shallow serving dish.
2. In a small bowl, combine oil, lemon juice, sugar, salt, oregano, and parsley mix well.
3. Pour oil mixture over tomatoes; cover, and refrigerate for at least 3 hours to marinate.
Serves: 8 - 10

MOZZARELLA AND TOMATO SALAD

Simple and fresh – my favorite kind of side dish! This one can also be used as a lovely appetizer.

6 ounces fresh Mozzarella cheese, cut into ¼-inch slices
4 medium tomatoes, peeled and sliced
¼ cup fresh basil leaves, finely chopped
⅓ cup olive oil
2 tablespoons white wine vinegar
½ teaspoon sugar
salt and pepper to taste

1. In a medium sized shallow serving dish, layer Mozzarella, tomatoes, and basil.
2. In a small bowl, add oil, vinegar, sugar, salt, and pepper; whisk to combine.
3. Pour oil mixture over Mozzarella and tomatoes; cover, refrigerate to chill.
Serves: 6

PEA SALAD

The red onion, dill, and fresh lemon juice combine to make this salad flavorsome. Remember, if even finely chopped onion is problematic for you, replace the onion with a half teaspoon or so of onion powder.

1 (16-ounce) package frozen peas
¼ cup red onion, finely chopped
1 cup cheddar cheese, shredded
3 hard cooked eggs, finely chopped
½ cup mayonnaise
¼ cup sour cream
1 tablespoon lemon juice
1½ teaspoons dill weed
½ teaspoon salt
½ teaspoon black pepper

1. Cook peas according to package directions, or until tender; drain; refrigerate to chill.
2. In a large bowl, combine chilled peas, onion, cheese, and eggs.
3. In a small bowl, whisk together mayonnaise, sour cream, lemon juice, dill, salt and pepper.
4. Pour mayonnaise mixture over pea mixture; stir gently to combine.
5. Cover; refrigerate to chill.
Serves: 4 - 6

Potato Salad

A traditional summer side dish, I usually put several hard boiled eggs in it as my parents sometimes eat a small dish of potato salad as a simple lunch. I use veggie bacon because it becomes soft in salad dressing while still giving that lovely bacon taste.

4 medium potatoes, cooked, peeled, and diced
4 hard cooked eggs, peeled and chopped
2 pieces veggie bacon, crisp cooked and crumbled
1 teaspoon onion powder
½ cup mayonnaise
¼ cup Ranch dressing
1½ teaspoons vinegar
2 teaspoons sugar
1 teaspoon prepared mustard
1 tablespoon chives
1 tablespoon Parmesan cheese, grated
½ teaspoon seasoned salt
¼ teaspoon black pepper

1. In a large bowl, place cooled diced potatoes, chopped eggs, and veggie bacon crumbles.
2. In a medium bowl, add mayonnaise, Ranch dressing, vinegar, sugar, chives, Parmesan cheese, seasoned salt and pepper; stir until well blended.
3. Pour mayonnaise dressing mixture over potato mixture; stir gently to combine; cover, refrigerate.
Serves: 6 - 8

Soft Cauliflower Salad

A lovely, light soft salad. You can also substitute your favorite salad dressing for the dressing used here.

4 cups water
3 cups cauliflower florets
1 bay leaf

Dressing
⅓ cup olive oil
1 clove garlic, finely chopped
2 tablespoons balsamic or white wine vinegar
½ teaspoon sugar
½ teaspoon basil
½ teaspoon oregano
⅛ teaspoon thyme or rosemary
⅛ teaspoon black pepper

1. In a medium saucepan, bring 4 cups water to a boil; add cauliflower and bay leaf.
2. Cover, cook over low heat until cauliflower is soft; drain, remove bay leaf; place cauliflower in a medium bowl and refrigerate to cool.
3. Meanwhile, in a small bowl, combine olive oil, garlic, vinegar, sugar, basil, oregano, thyme, and pepper; whisk until well blended.
4. Drizzle dressing over cauliflower; toss gently to combine; cover and refrigerate to chill.
Serves: 4

SUMMER FRUIT SALAD

You can't go wrong with fresh fruit. No dressing is needed, as fresh fruit is flavorful by itself. This salad bowl will empty quickly.

2 cups cantaloupe, cubed
2 cups watermelon, cubed
2 cups strawberries, halved
2 bananas, cut into 1-inch slices
½ cup blueberries

1. Place cantaloupe, watermelon, strawberries, and bananas in large bowl.
2. Gently toss fruit together.
3. Sprinkle blueberries on top.
4. Serve.
Serves: 12

TRADITIONAL DEVILED EGGS

To suit your family's tastes, you can add flavorful herbs and spices to this basic recipe, such as curry powder, horseradish, chives, or finely chopped olives.

6 hard-cooked eggs, peeled
3 tablespoons mayonnaise
1 teaspoon sugar
1 teaspoon white vinegar
1 teaspoon prepared mustard
¼ teaspoon salt
⅛ teaspoon black pepper
paprika

1. Cut eggs in half lengthwise; remove the yolks to a small bowl, and place the egg whites side by side in a serving dish, with cut side up.

2. In a small bowl, mash the yolks with a fork; add mayonnaise, sugar, vinegar, mustard, salt and pepper; mix well.

3. Spoon the yolk mixture into the egg whites; sprinkle with paprika.

4. Cover; refrigerate to chill.

Serves: 12

TUNA AND BEAN SALAD

Tuna and beans? Try it! You'll be pleasantly surprised. This chilled, light salad is especially enjoyable on a warm summer day.

1 (12-ounce) can solid white tuna, drained

¼ cup green onions, finely chopped, or ½ teaspoon onion powder

1 (15-ounce) can navy or great northern beans, rinsed and drained

1½ tablespoons fresh parsley, finely chopped

⅓ cup mayonnaise or slaw dressing

½ teaspoon celery seeds

2 tablespoons lemon juice

1½ tablespoons olive oil

¼ teaspoon oregano or rosemary

¼ teaspoon black pepper

1. In a medium bowl, combine tuna, onions, and beans.

2. In a small bowl, combine parsley, mayonnaise, celery seeds, lemon juice, olive oil, oregano and pepper; stir or whisk until well blended.

3. Pour mayonnaise mixture over tuna mixture; toss gently to combine.

4. Cover; refrigerate to chill.

Serves: 6

HOT SIDE DISHES

APPLE NOODLES

The recipe for this delightfully different side dish can easily be doubled to serve a group, such as for brunch or to take to a potluck dinner.

1 (8-ounce) package noodles
2 tablespoons butter
2 eggs, lightly beaten
¼ cup sugar
½ cup sour cream
1 cup small-curd cottage cheese
¼ cup milk
½ teaspoon vanilla
1 medium to large cooking apple, shredded
1 teaspoon cinnamon sugar (optional)

Heat oven to 350 degrees

1. Cook noodles according to package instructions.
2. Transfer drained noodles to large bowl; add butter to noodles; stirring until butter is melted and noodles are coated.
3. Add eggs, sugar, sour cream, cottage cheese, milk, vanilla and apple; mix well.
4. Pour mixture into a greased 8x8-inch baking dish.
5. Sprinkle with cinnamon sugar if desired.
6. Cover; bake in a 350 degree oven for 30 minutes, or until set.
Serves: 6

BAKED ACORN SQUASH

This dish is so tender, so tasty, so easy to make, and looks pretty, too – the best of all worlds.

2 acorn squash
4 teaspoons butter
4 tablespoons maple syrup

Heat oven to 350 degrees

1. Cut each squash in half lengthwise; remove seeds and any fibrous material.
2. In a 9x13-inch baking dish, place squash halves side by side, with cut side up.
3. Place 1 teaspoon butter and 1 tablespoon maple syrup into each half.
4. Bake at 350 degrees for 1 hour, or until soft.
Serves: 4

BROCCOLI AND PASTA

You can use noodles or any pasta of your choice for this colorful Italian dish.

1 (8-ounce) package egg noodles
2 tablespoons olive oil
2 tablespoons green onion, finely chopped
2 cups broccoli florets, finely chopped
1 (14-ounce) can diced tomatoes, undrained
½ teaspoon oregano
½ teaspoon thyme
½ teaspoon black pepper
2 tablespoons Parmesan cheese, grated

1. Cook noodles according to package directions; drain.
2. Meanwhile, in a medium skillet, add oil and onion; cook over medium heat until onion is softened, about 5 minutes.
3. Add broccoli, tomatoes with their juice, oregano, thyme, and pepper; stir.
4. Cover; cook over low heat until broccoli is tender, about 20 minutes.
5. Stir in cooked noodles; continue cooking until heated throughout; top with Parmesan cheese before serving.
Serves: 4

CABBAGE AND NOODLES

This is another of our family favorites, made countless times. I sometimes add finely chopped chicken to turn it into a one-dish meal.

1 (8-ounce) package egg noodles
2 tablespoons butter or olive oil
1 cup onion, finely chopped
2 cloves garlic, finely chopped
4 cups green cabbage, chopped or shredded
1½ teaspoons seasoned salt
¼ teaspoon black pepper
¼-½ cup chicken broth

1. Cook noodles according to package directions; drain.

2. Meanwhile, in a large skillet, heat butter or olive oil over medium heat; add onion and garlic, cooking until softened, about 5 minutes.

3. Add cabbage, seasoned salt, pepper and ¼ cup broth; stir occasionally, adding more broth if needed to retain moisture.

4. Cover; cook over low heat until cabbage is tender, about 30 minutes.

5. Add cooked noodles to cabbage mixture; mix well, stirring until heated throughout.

Serves: 6 - 8

CANDIED SWEET POTATOES

This is a quick stovetop version of the traditional baked candied sweet potatoes.

6 medium sweet potatoes, cooked whole and peeled
2 tablespoons butter
⅔ cup brown sugar
½ cup water
salt to taste

1. Cut cooked, peeled potatoes in half lengthwise; set aside.
2. In a large skillet, melt butter over medium heat; add sugar and stir until sugar is melted.
3. Add water; stir and bring to a boil.
4. Place the sweet potatoes in the skillet, flat-side down, on top of the syrup; cook slowly over low heat, turning so both sides are coated with syrup and warmed throughout.
Serves: 6

CARROT PATTIES

Try adding a dollop of warmed applesauce on top before serving for even more flavor and softness.

2 eggs, lightly beaten
3 cups carrots, cooked, mashed, and any fibrous pieces removed
3 tablespoons butter, melted
⅓ cup all-purpose or light baking flour
2 teaspoons baking powder
½ cup milk
1 tablespoon butter

1. In a large bowl, combine eggs, mashed carrots, butter, flour, baking powder, and milk.
2. In a large skillet, melt one-half tablespoon butter; pour one-fourth cup of batter into skillet to form each patty, flatting, if needed, to form into patties.
3. Cook on low heat about 3 minutes on each side, or until browned. Repeat step 2 for remaining batter.
Serves: 4

CARROT SOUFFLÉ

A light and smooth dish, this makes a great side dish for either formal or informal meals.

2 cups carrots, peeled and cut into slices
¼ cup butter, softened
3 eggs
1 cup milk
⅓ cup sugar
3 tablespoons all-purpose flour
1 teaspoon baking powder
½ teaspoon vanilla
½ teaspoon cinnamon

Heat oven to 350 degrees

1. In a small saucepan, cook carrots in water until tender; drain.
2. Place carrots in a blender, pulse to soften; add butter, eggs, milk, sugar, flour, baking powder, vanilla, and cinnamon. Blend until smooth.
3. Pour into a greased 8x8-inch casserole dish; bake at 350 degrees for 40 minutes, or until knife inserted in center comes out clean.
Serves: 6

CREAMED PEAS

For a softer dish yet, puree just before serving.

⅔ cup chicken broth
2 cups green peas, fresh or frozen
2 tablespoons butter
⅓ cup half-and-half
2 tablespoons flour
¼ teaspoon black pepper
¼ teaspoon salt
2 tablespoons Parmesan cheese, grated (optional)

1. In a medium saucepan, add broth and peas; bring to near boiling. Reduce heat.
2. Cover; cook on low heat 25 minutes, or until peas are tender. Add butter.
3. In a small bowl, combine half-and-half and flour; add to the peas mixture, cook and stir until thickened.
4. Add the pepper and salt, plus Parmesan cheese if desired, stirring to combine.
Serves: 4

CREAMED SPINACH

This is a traditional recipe for creamed spinach—the kind you remember from days gone by.

2 (10-ounce) packages frozen spinach, thawed, finely chopped
2 tablespoons butter
1 small clove garlic, finely chopped
2 tablespoons onion, finely chopped

Sauce
2 tablespoons butter
2 tablespoons all-purpose flour
1 cup milk
¼ teaspoon salt
⅛ teaspoon black pepper
⅛ teaspoon nutmeg

1. Cook spinach according to package directions.
2. Meanwhile, in a small skillet, melt butter over medium heat; add onion and garlic; stir and cook until softened, about 5 minutes. Add spinach; stir gently to combine and transfer to a serving bowl.
3. Meanwhile, in a small saucepan, melt butter over low heat; add flour, milk, salt, pepper, and nutmeg; stir until thickened to desired consistency.
4. Pour sauce over spinach; stir to combine. Serve.
Serves: 8

FETTUCCINE ALFREDO

This side dish is a little on the rich side due to the cream and butter, but if you don't need to worry about calories – or need to add calories to your diet – this is a side dish that is so tasty and so simple to make, you can't go wrong.

6-ounces fettuccine, uncooked
½ cup light cream
1 tablespoon butter
½ cup fresh Parmesan cheese, grated
black pepper

1. In a medium saucepan, cook fettuccine according to package directions; drain; return to saucepan.
2. Add light cream, butter and Parmesan cheese; stir until butter is melted and fettuccine is well coated.
3. Sprinkle with black pepper; serve.
Serves: 4

FRIED POTATOES

This is a side dish that I make often. It is easy to make, flavorful, and goes beautifully with most sandwiches or omelets.

2 tablespoons olive oil
1 small onion, finely chopped
1 clove garlic, thinly sliced
1 medium potato, peeled, thinly sliced
salt and pepper to taste
¼ cup water
catsup (optional)

1. In a medium skillet, heat oil.

2. Add onion, garlic, potato slices, salt and pepper; stir to combine.

3. Pour water over top; cover, and cook over low heat under tender, about 20 minutes, stirring occasionally. Add more water if needed to remain moist while cooking.

4. When potatoes are soft, uncover and continue cooking until the potatoes begin to lightly brown on one side; turn over to brown other side.

5. Serve with catsup if desired.

Serves: 1

GARDEN VEGETABLE BAKE

You may need to pre-cook the onion for even more softness before adding to this dish. Either the microwave or stovetop will do the trick. You can substitute the vegetables used in this recipe for your favorite soft vegetables.

1 cup zucchini, peeled, chopped
1 cup tomatoes, peeled, chopped
½ cup onion, finely chopped
⅓ cup Cheddar cheese, shredded
2 eggs, lightly beaten
½ cup baking mix
1 cup milk
½ teaspoon salt
¼ teaspoon black pepper

Heat oven to 375 degrees

1. In a greased pie dish, layer zucchini, tomatoes, onion, and cheese.
2. In a medium bowl, combine eggs, baking mix, milk, salt, and pepper; mix well, and pour into pie dish over vegetables.
3. Bake in a 375 degree oven for 30 minutes, or until a knife inserted in center comes out clean.
Serves: 6 - 8

GNOCCHI IN CREAM SAUCE

You can enjoy this recipe as a simple side dish or create a more colorful, dashing dish by adding soft vegetables to the sauce, such as chopped olives, diced tomatoes, cooked peas, or finely chopped spinach.

1 (12-ounce) package potato gnocchi
⅔ cup half-and-half
2 ounces cream cheese, diced
½ teaspoon salt
½ teaspoon garlic powder
¼ teaspoon oregano
¼ teaspoon basil
¼ teaspoon black pepper

1. Cook gnocchi according to package directions; drain.

2. Meanwhile, in a saucepan add half-and-half, cream cheese, salt, garlic powder, oregano, basil and pepper; cook over medium heat until heated throughout and cream cheese is melted, about 10 minutes. Add ½ cup cooked soft vegetable, if desired.

3. Place cooked gnocchi in serving dish; pour cream sauce over gnocchi.

Serves: 4

HOT GERMAN POTATO SALAD

Using veggie bacon in place of regular bacon allows this dish to have the bacon taste without the crunch, as veggie bacon becomes soft in this dish. And it is a good source of protein, too.

¼ cup olive oil
½ cup onions, finely chopped
2 tablespoons all-purpose flour
2 tablespoons sugar
½ teaspoon celery seeds
½ teaspoon salt
⅛ teaspoon black pepper
½ cup cider vinegar
¾ cup water
6 medium potatoes, cooked, peeled, thinly sliced
4 -5 slices veggie bacon, cooked, crumbled

1. Heat oil in a large skillet; add onions and cook until softened, about 5 minutes.
2. Add flour, sugar, celery seeds, salt, pepper and vinegar; continue stirring until mixture boils.
3. Add potatoes and bacon, stirring until well combined; serve.
Serves: 6

POLENTA

To ensure softness, be sure to buy finely ground cornmeal, rather than the more coarsely ground cornmeal commonly used in polenta. Adding a half cup grated Parmesan cheese adds flavor as well as protein, and you can also replace some of the water with milk for a creamier polenta.

4 cups water
1 cup yellow cornmeal
1 teaspoon salt
butter
½ cup Parmesan cheese, grated (optional)

1. In a medium saucepan, add water and bring to a boil.
2. Slowly stir in cornmeal; add salt. Continue stirring until thickened, about 10 minutes.
3. Cover; cook over low heat for 5 minutes, or until very thick.
4. Pour polenta into greased 9x5-inch loaf pan; cover and refrigerate to chill.
5. When chilled, turn pan upside down to remove polenta; cut into ½-inch slices.
6. In a large skillet, melt butter; place polenta slices side by side in skillet and cook until lightly browned on one side, then flip over to brown other side.
Serves: 6

POTATO CAKES

This is a wonderful way of using leftover mashed potatoes. They make a nice side dish to accompany a sandwich.

2 cups mashed potatoes
1 egg, lightly beaten
1 tablespoon all-purpose flour
2 tablespoons half-and-half
¼ teaspoon garlic powder
1 tablespoon onion, finely chopped, or ¼ teaspoon onion powder
2 tablespoons butter

1. In a medium bowl, mix together potatoes, egg, flour, half-and-half, garlic powder and onion.

2. In a large skillet, melt butter to coat skillet bottom.

3. Form potato mixture into patties; place patties into hot skillet.

4. Cook until lightly browned; flip over and brown other side. Serve.

Serves: 4 – 6

REFRIED BEANS

After adding the liquid it may take awhile to cook down to your desired consistency. That's what you want—the longer it cooks the softer it gets.

2 tablespoons olive oil
½ cup onion, finely chopped
1 clove garlic, finely chopped
1 (15-ounce) can pinto beans, rinsed and drained
¾ cup water or chicken broth
1 teaspoon salt

1. In a medium skillet, heat oil over medium heat; add onion and garlic and cook until softened, about 5 minutes.
2. In a separate bowl, mash beans; add half of beans to skillet. Stir and cook until heated through.
3. Add remaining beans, water or broth, and salt.
4. Stir and cook over low heat until of desired consistency.
Serves: 4

SCALLOPED CARROTS

I use my mini-food processor to slice the carrots. They are nice and thin, and cook up soft in minutes.

4 cups carrots, peeled and thinly sliced
1 medium onion, finely chopped
6 tablespoons butter, divided
2 cups whole milk
3 tablespoons flour
½ teaspoon salt
¼ teaspoon black pepper
½ cup butter-style cracker crumbs

Heat oven to 350 degrees

1. In a medium saucepan, cook carrots in boiling water until tender; drain.
2. Meanwhile, in a medium skillet melt one tablespoon butter over medium heat; add onions and cook until softened, about 5 minutes. Stir in cooked carrots and remove from heat.
3. In a medium saucepan, melt 3 tablespoons butter over medium heat then mix with flour, salt and pepper; slowly whisk in milk, continue whisking until thickened.
4. Place carrot mixture into a 1½-quart casserole dish; pour sauce over the carrots.
5. In a small bowl, combine cracker crumbs with 2 tablespoons melted butter; sprinkle evenly over casserole.
6. Bake in a 350 degree oven for 30 minutes, or until bubbly.
Serves: 8

Spaghetti in Tomato Sauce

A simple homemade tomato sauce with spaghetti noodles makes a tasty and filling side dish for many main dishes. Or turn it into a main dish by adding some cooked ground beef while it simmers.

2 tablespoons olive oil
½ cup onion, finely chopped
2 cloves garlic, minced
1 (14-ounce) can diced tomatoes, with juice
½ teaspoon black pepper
¼ teaspoon salt
½ teaspoon oregano
½ teaspoon basil
4-ounces spaghetti, uncooked

1. In a medium skillet, heat oil; add onion and garlic and cook until softened, about 5 minutes.
2. Add diced tomatoes with juice, salt, pepper, oregano and basil; cover and simmer over low heat.
3. Meanwhile, cook spaghetti according to package instructions; drain.
4. Add spaghetti to tomato mixture; continue cooking over low heat until spaghetti has absorbed some the of tomato juice. Serve.
Serves: 4

SPANISH RICE

This is an attractive, appetizing side dish that only takes a few steps, and few ingredients, to make.

2 tablespoons olive oil
1 cup onions, finely chopped
½ cup green peppers, finely chopped
1 (8-ounce) can tomato sauce
½ teaspoon black pepper
½ teaspoon salt
1½ teaspoons garlic powder
5 cups white rice, cooked

1. In a large skillet, heat oil; add onions and green peppers, cook over low heat until softened, about 5 minutes.
2. Add tomato sauce, pepper, salt, and garlic powder; cover, cook over low heat for 10 minutes, or until onions are soft.
3. Stir in rice; cooking on low heat until heated throughout, about 3 minutes.
Serves: 8

STEWED TOMATOES

For the tomato lover, this simple tomato recipe is sure to please.

2 pounds tomatoes
¼ cup onion, finely chopped
2 teaspoons sugar
1½ tablespoons butter
salt and pepper to taste

1. Peel tomatoes, remove cores, and cut into quarters.
2. In a medium saucepan, add tomatoes and onions; cover, cook until onions are softened, about 15 minutes; stirring occasionally.
3. Add sugar, butter, salt, and pepper; stir until butter is melted. Serve.
Serves: 4

SUMMER SQUASH IN CHEESE SAUCE

This lovely cheese sauce is mild in flavor and smooth in texture. A perfect sauce for any of your favorite soft vegetables.

2 pounds summer squash, such as zucchini, peeled and cut into ½-inch slices

2 tablespoons butter

2 tablespoons all-purpose flour

1 cup milk

1 cup Cheddar cheese, shredded

½ teaspoon Worcestershire sauce

¼ teaspoon black pepper

¼ teaspoon paprika (optional)

1. In a medium saucepan, cook squash slices in near boiling water until soft; drain.

2. Meanwhile, in a small saucepan, melt butter; stir in flour, blend well and remove from heat.

3. Add milk slowly to flour mixture, stirring constantly until smooth; return to heat and continue stirring until thickened.

4. Remove from heat; add cheese and stir until melted.

5. Stir in Worcestershire sauce, salt, and pepper, and paprika if desired.

6. Place cooked squash slices in a serving dish; pour cheese sauce over them.

Serves: 4 – 6

SWEET POTATO CASSEROLE

Beating with an electric mixer whips this into a light and fluffy side dish.

4 medium sweet potatoes, peeled and quartered
⅓ cup brown sugar
1 egg, lightly beaten
1 teaspoon vanilla extract
½ cup orange juice
1 cup marshmallows (optional)

Heat oven to 350 degrees

1. In a large saucepan, cook potatoes in lightly salted water until soft; drain.
2. Using an electric mixer, beat sweet potatoes until smooth.
3. Add brown sugar, egg, vanilla, and orange juice; beat well.
4. Pour mixture into a greased 1½-quart baking dish.
5. Cover; bake in a 350 degree oven for 35 minutes; top with marshmallows, if desired, and bake uncovered another 5 minutes to brown marshmallows.
Serves: 6 - 8

Tasty Green Beans

The small amount of sugar in this recipe makes a big difference in taste. Lovely.

2 tablespoons olive oil
1 small clove garlic, finely chopped
¼ cup onion, finely chopped
1 (14½-ounce) can cut green beans, drained
1 teaspoon sugar
¼ teaspoon salt
⅛ teaspoon black pepper
2 tablespoons water
2 tablespoons ham, finely chopped (optional)

1. In a medium skillet, heat oil; add garlic and onions, cooking until softened, about 5 minutes.
2. Add green beans, sugar, salt, pepper and water, plus ham if desired. Stir.
3. Cover; cook over low heat for 30 minutes, until green beans and onions are tender; stir occasionally.
Serves: 3 - 4

ZUCCHINI WITH TOMATOES

This wonderful combination of zucchini and tomatoes gives you the taste of summer all year round.

¼ cup olive oil
¾ cup onion, finely chopped
1 clove garlic, finely chopped
3 medium zucchini, peeled, thinly sliced
1 (28-ounce) can tomatoes, chopped
1 teaspoon salt
¼ teaspoon black pepper
¼ teaspoon oregano

1. In a large skillet, heat olive oil over medium heat; add onion and garlic, cooking until softened, about 5 minutes.
2. Stir in zucchini, tomatoes, salt, pepper and oregano; cover and cook over low heat until zucchini is tender, stirring occasionally.
Serves: 8

SANDWICHES

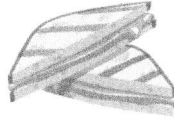

Chicken Salad Sandwich   180
Curried Chicken Salad Sandwich   181
Denver Sandwich   182
Egg Salad Sandwich   183
Fried Bologna Sandwich   184
Grilled Cheese and Tomato Sandwich   185
Ham and Swiss Sandwich   186
Ham Salad Sandwich   187
Hot Shredded Chicken Sandwich   188
Kentucky Hot Brown Sandwich   189
Open-faced Pizza Burgers   191
Pimento Cheese Sandwich   192
Saucy Chicken Crescent Rolls 193
Sausage Sandwich with Onion & Peppers
  194
Shrimp Salad Sandwich   195
Sloppy Joe Sandwich   196
Slow Cooker Italian Sandwich   197
Slow Cooker Meatball Sandwich   198
Tuna Salad Sandwich   199
Turkey Burgers   200

CHICKEN SALAD SANDWICH

Deliciously soft and enjoyable to eat. Doesn't everyone love chicken salad? You can always spice it up by adding a little mustard, chili powder, or any of your favorite spices or herbs.

⅓ cup mayonnaise
½ teaspoon vinegar
½ teaspoon sugar
¼ teaspoon onion powder
¼ teaspoon garlic powder
salt and pepper to taste
1½ cups cooked chicken, finely chopped
4 hard cooked eggs, finely chopped
4 soft sandwich buns

1. In a medium bowl, combine mayonnaise, vinegar, sugar, onion powder, garlic powder, salt and pepper; stir until well blended.
2. Add chicken and eggs, mix gently to combine; cover and refrigerate to chill.
3. Spoon into sandwich buns to serve.
Serves: 4

CURRIED CHICKEN SALAD SANDWICH

This tasty chicken salad can be eaten as a simple cold salad as well as in a sandwich bun. If eaten as a salad, you may want to serve it with a homemade muffin, such as applesauce muffin, or any moist and tasty bread of your choice.

⅓ cup mayonnaise
⅓ cup vanilla yogurt
1 teaspoon lemon juice
½ teaspoon sweet curry powder
¼ teaspoon onion powder
¼ teaspoon celery seeds
2 cups cooked chicken breast, finely chopped
¼ cup green grapes, seedless, chopped
4 soft sandwich buns

1. In a medium bowl, combine mayonnaise, yogurt, lemon juice, curry powder, onion powder and celery seeds; stir until well blended.
2. Add chicken and grapes; mix gently.
3. Cover; refrigerate to chill.
4. Spoon chilled chicken salad into sandwich buns to serve.
Serves: 4

DENVER SANDWICH

This sandwich is very easy to make and full of flavor. At times my mother asks for just the egg patty without the bread to eat as a flavorful omelet-type egg patty along with pancakes or a piece of toast.

½ teaspoon butter
1 tablespoon onion, finely chopped
1 tablespoon green pepper, finely chopped
1 egg
1 tablespoon shaved ham, finely chopped
salt and pepper to taste
2 slices of soft bread, buttered if desired.

1. In a small skillet, melt butter; add onion and green pepper and cook over low heat until softened, about 5 minutes.

2. In a small bowl, beat egg with fork or whisk; add ham.

3. Pour egg mixture into the pan over onion and green pepper; sprinkle salt and pepper to taste.

4. Cook over low heat until nearly set, then flip over, cooking for another 30 seconds to set.

5. Serve between two slices of bread.

Serves: 1

EGG SALAD SANDWICH

A light and lovely classic egg salad sandwich. You can turn this into curried egg salad by adding ½ teaspoon sweet curry powder, or try adding some shredded cheese, cooked peas and finely crumbled bacon (veggie bacon is softer yet).

½ cup mayonnaise
2 tablespoons pickle relish
1 teaspoon prepared mustard
¼ teaspoon salt
¼ teaspoon black pepper
8 hard-cooked eggs, peeled and chopped
1 tomato, peeled and sliced (optional)
4 soft sandwich buns

1. In a medium bowl, combine mayonnaise, relish, mustard, salt and pepper.
2. Add chopped eggs; mix gently. Refrigerate to chill.
3. Spoon chilled egg salad into sandwich buns; top with tomato slices if desired.
Serves: 4

FRIED BOLOGNA SANDWICH

Many of us grew up with fried bologna sandwiches. It's definitely one of the easiest sandwiches to make.

1 slice of ¼-inch thick bologna or 2 slices prepackaged
  bologna
1 soft sandwich bun
catsup
mustard (optional)

1. Cut bologna from center of slice to outside edge, so it will lay flat in skillet.
2. Heat a small skillet over medium heat; place bologna in pan and cook until it begins to brown; turn over and cook other side until lightly browned.
3. Place fried bologna into bun; top with catsup, and mustard if desired.
Serves: 1

GRILLED CHEESE AND TOMATO SANDWICH

Use your favorite melty cheese to make this grilled cheese sandwich, and enjoy it with a bowl of your favorite soup. Such great comfort food!

8 slices of soft bread, crusts removed
4 tablespoons butter, softened
4 slices cheddar cheese
4 slices tomato, peeled and thinly sliced

1. Spread ½ tablespoon butter on one side of each slice of bread.

2. In a large skillet or griddle, place 4 slices of bread side by side, butter side down; top each with a slice of cheese and a tomato slice; top each with another bread slice, buttered side out.

3. Cook over low heat until one side is lightly browned, then flip over and cook other side until lightly browned and cheese is melty. Serve hot.

Serves: 4

HAM AND SWISS SANDWICH

Using ham with a smoked flavor enhances the taste of this very nice sandwich.

⅓ cup mayonnaise
1 teaspoon parsley flakes
½ teaspoon prepared mustard
¼ teaspoon onion powder
1 (5-ounce) can ground smoked ham, broken into small
    pieces
½ cup Swiss cheese, shredded
2 soft sandwich buns
2 tomato slices (optional)

1. In a medium bowl, combine mayonnaise, parsley, mustard, and onion powder; stir until well blended.
2. Add ham and cheese; mix just until combined. Refrigerate to chill.
3. Spoon ham and cheese mixture into sandwich buns; top with tomato slice, if desired.
Serves: 2

HAM SALAD SANDWICH

The smoked ham in this recipe turns a basic ham salad into a tasty sandwich.

2 (5-ounce) cans ground smoked ham, drained
2 hard cooked eggs, finely chopped
½ cup mayonnaise
2 tablespoons sweet pickle relish
½ teaspoon onion powder
1 teaspoon prepared mustard
¼ teaspoon black pepper
½ cup cheddar cheese, shredded (optional)
4 soft sandwich buns

1. In a medium bowl, break ham apart into small pieces; add eggs.
2. In a small bowl, combine mayonnaise, pickle relish, onion powder, mustard and pepper; stir until well blended.
3. Pour mayonnaise mixture over ham and eggs, adding cheese if desired. Mix well; refrigerate to chill.
4. Spoon ham salad into sandwich buns to serve.
Serves: 4

HOT SHREDDED CHICKEN SANDWICH

This family favorite is cooked in broth, while some hot shredded chicken recipes use a can of creamed soup to create a creamier sauce. If you prefer to use soup, just use half the amount of broth and leave out the seasoned salt. Either way, this is an enjoyable sandwich.

3½ cups cooked chicken, finely chopped or 1 (28-ounce) can chicken
1¾ cups chicken broth, divided
½ sleeve round buttery crackers, crushed
1 teaspoon seasoned salt
¼ teaspoon black pepper
1 (10¾-ounce) can low-sodium cream of mushroom soup (optional)
8 soft sandwich buns

1. In a medium saucepan, add chicken, 1½ cups broth, cracker crumbs, seasoned salt and pepper; stir and cook over low heat.

2. Continue cooking, stirring frequently, until heated throughout and chicken is moist and slightly juicy, but not so wet that it will make the buns soggy; add more broth if it becomes too dry while cooking.

3. Spoon hot chicken into sandwich buns; serve.

Serves: 6 - 8

KENTUCKY HOT BROWN SANDWICH

This is a soft version of Kentucky's classic open faced sandwich. Smothered in a rich cream sauce and placed under the broiler, it is as much a casserole as an open-faced sandwich. The veggie bacon becomes soft in the sauce, but go ahead and use regular bacon if you can eat a dish with a little crunch.

¼ cup butter
¼ cup all purpose flour
1 cup half-and-half
¾ cup milk
½ cup Parmesan cheese, grated
¼ teaspoon salt
¼ teaspoon black pepper
1½ cups turkey breast, finely chopped
2 slices Texas Toast or 1-inch slices of Italian bread, crusts trimmed
4 slices of crisp veggie bacon, crumbled
1 large tomato, peeled, diced
¼ cup cheddar cheese
1 tablespoon parsley, finely chopped

1. In a medium saucepan, melt butter; whisk in flour and blend until smooth.

2. Add half-and-half and milk; whisk until heated throughout and slightly thickened.

3. Add Parmesan cheese, salt and pepper to saucepan, whisking until cheese is melted; remove from heat.

4. Place bread slices in individual baking dishes (or both in one larger baking dish); top each slice with ¾ cup turkey and 2 slices of crumbled bacon.

5. Pour half of the cheese sauce over each turkey sandwich; sprinkle with diced tomatoes then cheddar cheese.

6. Place under broiler until cheddar cheese begins to brown, about 5 minutes.

7. Sprinkle chopped parsley over top. Serve.

Serves: 2

OPEN FACED PIZZA BURGERS

If this is too messy for you to pick up to eat, just pile the meat onto the buns until overflowing and your knife and fork will do the rest.

2 tablespoons vegetable oil
½ cup onion, finely chopped
2 cloves garlic, finely chopped
1 pound ground beef
¾ cup pizza sauce
½ teaspoon salt
¼ teaspoon black pepper
¼ teaspoon cinnamon
1 cup mozzarella cheese, shredded
6 soft sandwich buns

1. In a large skillet, heat oil; add onion and garlic, cook over low heat until softened, about 5 minutes.

2. Add ground beef; break beef apart with spoon as it cooks, until it becomes browned and crumbly. Drain fat.

3. Add pizza sauce, salt, pepper, and cinnamon; stir. Simmer for 10 minutes, or until heated throughout.

4. Spoon meat mixture into buns, topping with shredded cheese.

Serves: 6

PIMENTO CHEESE SANDWICH

This sandwich spread is easy to make and quite tasty. If you prefer a more intense taste, add a little more onion powder and garlic powder. You can even add a dash of cayenne pepper for an extra kick.

1 (3-ounce) package of cream cheese, softened
1 cup cheddar cheese, finely shredded
¼ cup mayonnaise
1 (2-ounce) jar pimento, drained, finely chopped
⅛ teaspoon garlic powder
¼ teaspoon onion powder
salt and pepper to taste
8 slices soft sandwich bread

1. In a medium bowl, place cream cheese; beat with an electric mixer until fluffy.
2. Add cheddar cheese, mayonnaise, pimento, garlic powder, onion powder, and salt and pepper to taste; continue beating until well combined. Refrigerate to chill.
3. Spread onto bread slices to serve.
Serves: 4

SAUCY CHICKEN CRESCENT ROLLS

This knife and fork sandwich may take a little extra work, but the effort is well worth it. Don't go past this one.

1 (3-ounce) package cream cheese, softened
2 tablespoons milk
⅛ teaspoon black pepper
1 tablespoon chives, finely chopped
1 tablespoon pimento, finely chopped
2 cups cooked chicken, finely chopped
1 (8-ounce) tube crescent rolls, refrigerated
1 (10¾-ounce) can cream of mushroom soup
½ soup can milk

Heat oven to 350 degrees

1. In a medium bowl, combine cream cheese, milk, pepper, chives and pimento; mix well. Stir in chicken.
2. Open tube of crescent rolls, separating into four squares; place on baking sheet one inch apart; seal perforations.
3. Spoon an equal amount of the chicken mixture into center of each square of crescent rolls; pull the four corners of each square up to center; seal.
4. Bake in a 350 degree oven for 20 minutes, or until lightly browned.
5. Meanwhile, in a small saucepan, combine soup and milk. Stir and cook over low heat until smooth and heated.
6. Spoon several tablespoons of the hot soup mixture over each serving.
Serves: 4

SAUSAGE SANDWICH WITH ONION & PEPPERS

Wonderfully simple and delightfully full of flavor. This sandwich will have them coming back for seconds.

2 tablespoons olive oil
1 large onion, finely chopped
1 large green pepper, seeded and finely chopped
⅛ cup water
1 (16-ounce) package skinless kielbasa sausage
6 soft sandwich buns

1. In a medium skillet, heat oil over medium heat; add onion and green pepper. Cook and stir over low heat until softened, about 5 minutes.
2. Add water and stir; cover and cook over low heat for 10 minutes, adding more water if needed to retain moisture.
3. Meanwhile, cut kielbasa into bite-size pieces. Add to skillet and stir; cover and cook over low heat for an additional 20 minutes, or until vegetables are tender and sausage is heated throughout.
4. Spoon mixture into sandwich buns to serve.
Serves: 6

SHRIMP SALAD SANDWICH

If you have a favorite shrimp sauce or salad dressing you can substitute that for the dressing ingredients listed below. Just follow your taste buds!

⅓ cup mayonnaise
½ teaspoon onion powder
¼ teaspoon dill
1 teaspoon vinegar or lemon juice
½ teaspoon sugar
⅛ teaspoon salt
2 (6-ounce) cans tiny shrimp, drained
2 hard cooked eggs, finely chopped
4 soft sandwich buns

1. In a medium bowl, combine mayonnaise, onion powder, dill, vinegar or lemon juice, sugar, and salt; stir or whisk until well blended.

2. Fold in eggs and shrimp.

3. Cover; refrigerate to chill.

4. Spoon chilled shrimp salad into buns to serve.

Serves: 2 - 4

Sloppy Joe Sandwich

A homemade Sloppy Joe recipe is so much better than the canned, pre-made sauce. And you can add seasonings to suit your own tastes. This is one my family likes.

1 tablespoon vegetable oil
½ cup onion, finely chopped
¼ cup green pepper, finely chopped
1 clove garlic, minced
1 pound ground beef
1 (8-ounce) can tomato sauce
¼ cup water or beef broth
1 teaspoon Worcestershire sauce
½ teaspoon paprika
½ teaspoon salt
¼ teaspoon black pepper
¼ teaspoon sugar
⅛ teaspoon celery seed powder
6 soft sandwich buns

1. In a large skillet, heat oil; cook onion, green pepper and garlic over low heat until softened, about 5 minutes.
2. Add ground beef; break beef apart with spoon as it cooks, until it becomes browned and crumbly. Drain fat.
3. Add tomato sauce, water or broth, Worcestershire sauce, paprika, salt, pepper, sugar and celery seed powder; stir.
4. Cover; simmer over low heat for 15 minutes, stirring occasionally.
5. Spoon mixture into buns to serve.
Serves: 6

SLOW COOKER ITALIAN SANDWICH

Lots of peppers, lots of flavor. This loose meat sandwich can easily be turned into an open faced sandwich for the daintier eater.

¾ pound ground beef
¾ pound bulk Italian sausage
1 large onion, finely chopped
1 large green pepper, finely chopped
1 large red or yellow pepper, finely chopped
½ teaspoon salt
½ teaspoon black pepper
1 (8-ounce) can tomato sauce
2 tablespoons tomato paste
1 cup mozzarella cheese, shredded
6 soft sandwich buns

1. In a large skillet, cook beef and sausage; break apart with spoon while cooking, until the meat becomes browned and crumbly. Drain fat.

2. Layer half of the onion and peppers in the slow cooker; top with half the meat mixture.

3. Sprinkle with salt and pepper; add remaining onion and peppers, top with remaining meat.

4. In a small bowl, combine tomato sauce and tomato paste; pour over meat mixture.

5. Cover; cook on Low for 5-6 hours, or until vegetables are tender.

6. Spoon mixture into buns; sprinkle some cheese onto each serving before placing the top bun.

Serves: 6

SLOW COOKER MEATBALL SANDWICH

This is such an easy sandwich to make, and so full of flavor. Whether your favorite is meatballs or pizza, this pizza flavored sandwich is sure to please.

1 (15-ounce) can pizza sauce
1½ pounds lean ground beef
½ cup dry bread crumbs, herb-seasoned
1 egg, lightly beaten
½ cup onions, finely chopped
¼ cup milk
6 soft sandwich buns

1. Spread half of the pizza sauce in the bottom of a slow cooker.
2. In a medium bowl, combine beef, bread crumbs, egg, onions, and milk. Mix well; form into 1½-inch meatballs.
3. Place meatballs in slow cooker; pour remaining pizza sauce over top. Cover; cook on Low heat for 6 hours.
4. Cut meatballs in half, if needed, and spoon meatballs and sauce into buns.
Serves: 6

TUNA SALAD SANDWICH

Tuna salad is a classic soft food and one of the easiest sandwiches to eat. It is versatile, too – try adding finely shredded cheese or a soft vegetable, such as cooked peas.

1 (6-ounce) can tuna, drained
2 hard cooked eggs, chopped
¼ cup mayonnaise
½ teaspoon prepared mustard
½ teaspoon onion powder
⅛ teaspoon salt
⅛ teaspoon black pepper
¼ teaspoon celery seeds
2 soft sandwich buns
2 tomato slices, peeled (optional)

1. In a medium bowl, break apart tuna; add chopped eggs.
2. In a small bowl, combine mayonnaise, mustard, onion powder, salt and pepper, and celery seed.
3. Pour mayonnaise mixture over tuna and eggs; mix well, refrigerate to chill.
4. Spoon chilled tuna salad into sandwich buns; top with tomato slice if desired.
Serves: 2

TURKEY BURGERS

These burgers are wonderfully moist. Top with your favorite burger toppings, or spoon the soup sauce on top. If biting into burgers is a problem, try eating them with a knife and fork, cutting them into bite size pieces.

⅓ cup milk
1 egg, lightly beaten
½ cup bread crumbs, herb-seasoned
1 pound ground turkey
¼ cup onion, finely chopped
½ teaspoon garlic powder
½ teaspoon salt
1 (10¾-ounce) can cream of mushroom soup
8 soft sandwich buns

1. In a medium bowl, beat milk and egg together. Add crumbs; stir and let sit 3 minutes to soften.
2. Add turkey, onion, garlic powder, and salt; mix well.
3. Shape into patties about ½-inch thick; set aside.
4. In a large skillet, spoon half of the can cream of mushroom soup evenly around bottom of skillet.
5. Place turkey patties side by side in skillet, spoon remaining soup on top. Cover; cook on medium heat for 15 minutes.
6. Flip to other side; cover and continue cooking for another 10 minutes, or until cooked throughout.
Serves: 8

SOUPS

BEEF BARLEY SOUP

A nourishing, hearty soup that really leaves you satisfied. Be sure to let this soup simmer for a couple hours so the barley becomes nice and tender. This soup will be even softer the second day, as the barley will continue to soften overnight.

1 pound ground beef
2 (14-ounce) cans beef broth
1 cup vegetable juice blend (such as V8)
4 cups water
1 cup carrots, peeled and thinly sliced
½ cup cabbage, finely shredded
½ cup green pepper, diced
1 cup onion, finely chopped
2 cloves garlic, minced
2 teaspoons seasoned salt
¾ cup barley, uncooked

1. In a large saucepan, cook ground beef, stirring until ground beef is browned and crumbly. Drain fat
2. Add broth, juice, water, carrots, cabbage, green pepper, onion, garlic, seasoned salt and barley; stir.
3. Cover; cook over low heat for 1½-2 hours, or until barley is tender; stir occasionally.
Serves: 6 - 8

BUTTERNUT SQUASH SOUP

This soup is a blended soup, very smooth and light with a lovely light taste. I enjoy a cup of this soup with a Cheesy-Chini Muffin (or two!) for a light and tasty lunch.

2 tablespoons olive oil
⅔ cup onions, finely chopped
1 cup carrots, thinly sliced
1 large potato, peeled, cubed
2 cups butternut squash, peeled, cubed
1 Granny Smith apple, peeled, cored, cubed
4 cups chicken broth
¼ teaspoon nutmeg
salt and pepper to taste
½ cup milk (optional)

1. In a medium saucepan, heat olive oil; add onions and cook over low heat until softened, about 5 minutes.

2. Add carrots, potato, squash, apple, and chicken broth; cover and cook over low heat until vegetables are tender, about 30 minutes. Stir in nutmeg, salt and pepper.

3. Place half the mixture into a blender; blend until smooth. Pour into another saucepan or large bowl and blend the remaining half of the vegetables until smooth.

4. Return to saucepan; stir in milk if desired. Serve.

Serves: 4 - 6

CHEESY CAULIFLOWER SOUP

My father doesn't like vegetables, but he always asks for seconds of this soup. Use homemade chicken broth whenever possible as it gives a richer flavor.

3 tablespoons olive oil
¾ cup onions, finely chopped
5 cups chicken broth
1 cup water
1 medium cauliflower, cut into florets
⅛ teaspoon rosemary
⅛ teaspoon thyme
¼ teaspoon black pepper
2 tablespoons butter, melted
¼ cup all-purpose flour
2 cups cheddar cheese, shredded

1. In a large saucepan, heat oil; add onions and cook over medium heat until softened, about 5 minutes.
2. Add broth, water, cauliflower, rosemary, thyme, and pepper. Cover; cook over low heat for 30 minutes, or until cauliflower is tender. Remove from heat.
3. Using a potato masher, mash cauliflower mixture until cauliflower is broken into small pieces; return to heat.
4. In a small bowl, combine melted butter and flour; mix well, then add to soup, cooking over low heat and stirring until soup is thickened to desired consistency.
5. Add cheese, one cup at a time, stirring until cheese is melted. Serve.
Serves: 6 - 8

Chicken Noodle Soup

Using home cooked chicken with homemade broth will add depth of flavor to this soup. Even if you only have one cup of homemade broth to add along with canned broth it will help create that homemade flavor for this lovely "comfort" soup.

1 tablespoon olive or canola oil
¾ cup onion, finely chopped
⅔ cup carrots, shredded
4 cups chicken broth
2 cups water
1 tablespoon dried celery flakes
1 bay leaf
1 cup cooked chicken, finely chopped
1 tablespoon parsley flakes
1 teaspoon seasoned salt
¼ teaspoon black pepper, or to taste
1½ cups egg noodles, uncooked and broken into 3-inch pieces

1. In a large saucepan, heat oil; add onion and carrots; cook over medium heat until they begin to soften, about 5 minutes.
2. Add broth, water, celery flakes, bay leaf, and chicken; cover and cook over low heat for 1 hour, stirring occasionally.
3. Stir in parsley, seasoned salt, pepper, and noodles; cover and continue cooking over low heat for 25 minutes. Remove bay leaf before serving.

Serves: 6 - 8

CHICKEN RICE AND BEAN SOUP

This soup was love at first bite for me. It's one to make over and over again. I usually use veggie bacon in place of regular bacon as it becomes soft in soup.

1 tablespoon olive oil
½ cup onion, finely chopped
1 clove garlic, finely chopped
1 (14½-ounce) can chicken broth, with roasted vegetable and herb flavoring*
½ cup water
1 cup canned great northern beans, rinsed and drained
¼ cup white or brown rice, cooked
¾ cup chicken, cooked and finely chopped
¼ teaspoon black pepper
1 strip bacon, cooked and finely crumbled

1. In a medium saucepan, heat oil; add onion and garlic, cooking over low heat until softened, about 5 minutes.
2. Add broth and water to saucepan; bring to near boiling; reduce heat.
3. Add remaining ingredients; cover and cook over low heat for 30 minutes. Stir occasionally.
Serves: 2 - 4

*If you can't find chicken broth with roasted garlic and herbs, use a can of plain chicken broth and add garlic and your favorite soup herbs. I use a dash of rosemary, thyme, oregano and a little red bell pepper. You may prefer basil, parsley, a bay leaf, etc.

CLAM CHOWDER

When choosing bacon be sure to use mild, or unflavored, bacon. A strong bacon, such as hickory smoked, can overpower the taste of the clam chowder.

1 cup onion, finely chopped
3 cups potatoes, diced
1 clove garlic, finely chopped
2 slices bacon, cooked and finely crumbled
1 teaspoon salt
¼ teaspoon black pepper
1 (8-ounce) bottle clam juice
2 (7-ounce) cans minced clams
3 tablespoons flour
1 cup milk
2 cups half-and-half

1. In a large saucepan, combine onion, potatoes, garlic, bacon, salt, pepper, and clam juice; cover and cook on low for 30 minutes, or until vegetables are soft.

2. In a small bowl, stir flour into milk; mix well.

3. Add flour and milk mixture to saucepan along with half-and-half and clams with their liquid; stirring constantly, cook over medium heat until chowder thickens to desired consistency.

4. Transfer the mixture to a blender; blend until smooth, and return to saucepan.

Serves: 6

CREAM OF BROCCOLI SOUP

If you love broccoli, this is the soup for you. Blended smooth, it goes down easy, is flavorful, and goes great with your favorite sandwich.

4 cups broccoli florets
1 cup onion, chopped
1 tablespoon celery flakes
1 clove garlic, chopped
1 medium potato, peeled and diced
1 (14-ounce) chicken broth
2 cups milk
1½ cups cheddar cheese, shredded
¼ teaspoon thyme
½ teaspoon salt
¼ teaspoon white pepper

1. In a medium saucepan, add broccoli, onion, celery flakes, garlic, potato, and chicken broth; bring to near boiling; reduce heat, cover and cook over low heat for 30 minutes, or until vegetables are soft.
2. Transfer cooked vegetables with broth to a blender; blend until smooth.
3. Return blended vegetables to saucepan; add milk, cheese, thyme, salt, and pepper.
4. Continue cooking over low heat until cheese is melted, stirring constantly.
Serves: 6

CREAM OF POTATO SOUP

This wonderfully versatile recipe can be easily changed to accommodate your tastes. It can be enjoyed as a simple potato soup, or other ingredients can be added, such as ham, cheese, or vegetables. For a smoother soup, just put it in a blender to puree or mash lightly.

1 tablespoon butter
1 cup onion, finely chopped
3 cups diced potatoes
3 cups chicken broth
¼ teaspoon black pepper
½ teaspoon salt
½ teaspoon garlic powder
¼ cup all-purpose flour
1½ cups milk
1 cup sharp cheddar cheese, shredded (optional)

1. In a medium saucepan, melt butter over medium heat. Add onion; stir and cook until onions are softened.
2. Add potatoes, chicken broth, pepper, salt, and garlic powder, plus ham if desired.
3. Cover; cook over low heat until potatoes are tender and easily fall apart, about 40 minutes.
4. In a small bowl, combine flour and milk; mix until smooth. Stir flour mixture into soup; continue cooking and stirring until soup is thickened and of desired consistency.
5. Add cheese if desired; stir just until melted and smooth. Serve.

Serves: 6

CREAMY CHICKEN VEGETABLE SOUP

This recipe was given to me by a dental assistant—she often made this soup for her in-laws when they began needing soft foods. They loved it, and so will you!

2 tablespoons olive oil
½ cup onions, finely chopped
½ cup carrots, thinly sliced or shredded
½ cup potatoes, diced
½ cup green beans
½ cup peas
1 cup chicken, finely chopped
1 (14-ounce) can chicken broth
¼ teaspoon black pepper
1¼ cups milk
1 (10¾-ounce) can cream of celery soup
1 (10¾-ounce) can cream of cheddar cheese soup

1. In a large saucepan, heat oil; add onions and carrots; cook and stir until softened, about 5 minutes.
2. Add potatoes, green beans, peas, chicken, broth, and pepper. Cover, and cook over low heat for 1½ hours, or until vegetables are soft; stir occasionally.
3. Add milk, celery soup and cheddar cheese soup; stir and continue cooking until heated throughout.
Serves: 6

FRENCH ONION SOUP

French onion soup has such great flavor, yet has only a few ingredients. This soup is wonderfully easy to throw together for a quick lunch.

1 tablespoon olive oil
2 cups sweet onions, finely chopped
4 cups beef broth
½ cup dry red wine
1 teaspoon garlic, finely chopped
6 slices French bread, 1-inch thick
6 tablespoons Parmesan cheese, freshly grated

1. In a large saucepan, add olive oil and onions; cook over medium heat, stirring often, until onions are browned.
2. Add broth, wine, and garlic; cover and cook over low heat for 25 minutes.
3. Meanwhile, toast bread until lightly browned; place one piece of toast in bottom of individual soup bowls; sprinkle each toast with 1 tablespoon Parmesan cheese.
4. Pour soup over toast to serve.
Serves: 6

HAM AND BEAN SOUP

You can never go wrong by warming up with this classic soup on a cold day. Eating it with corn bread on the side makes for a perfect, simple, meal.

½ (16-ounce) package navy beans
2 (14-ounce) cans chicken broth
2 cups water
1 cup carrots, thinly sliced
1 cup onion, finely chopped
2 cloves garlic, sliced
1 (14-ounce) can diced tomatoes, with juice
½ teaspoon black pepper
1½ teaspoons seasoned salt
1 cup green cabbage, finely chopped
1 (5-ounce) can smoked ground ham

1. Wash navy beans according to package directions.
2. In a large saucepan, heat 1 quart water to boiling. Remove from heat; add beans, cover and let sit for one hour to soften; drain.
3. Add broth, water, carrots, onion, garlic, tomatoes, pepper, seasoned salt, cabbage, and ham. Cover; cook on low heat for 3-4 hours, or until beans become very soft. Stir occasionally.
4. Using a potato masher, mash beans until about half of them are broken apart; stir to blend.
Serves: 8

KIELBASA AND BEAN SOUP WITH SPINACH

Smoked Kielbasa gives this soup a hearty flavor while the chopped fresh spinach gives it eye appeal.

4 ounces (½-large link) skinless smoked kielbasa
2 cups chicken broth
½ cup water
1 (14-ounce) can navy beans, rinsed and drained
½ cup onion, finely chopped
½ teaspoon basil
1 clove garlic, minced
1½ cups fresh spinach leaves

1. Cut kielbasa into ½ inch slices.

2. In a large saucepan, combine all ingredients except spinach; bring to near boiling, reduce heat, cover, and cook over low heat for 1 hour, or until beans are tender; stir occasionally.

3. Meanwhile, remove stems from spinach leaves; finely chop leaves by stacking one leaf on top of another, then slicing through the stack several times, lengthwise and crosswise.

4. Add chopped spinach, stir and cook an additional 10 minutes, or until spinach is softened.

Serves: 2 - 4

LOADED BAKED POTATO SOUP

The ingredients in this recipe blend into a flavorful, hearty treat of a soup. This recipe replaces regular bacon with veggie bacon for an even softer soup. The cheddar cheese can either be stirred into the soup or sprinkled on top of each serving, whichever you prefer.

2 tablespoons butter
1 cup onion, finely chopped
¼ cup red bell pepper, finely chopped
2 cloves garlic, finely chopped
2 tablespoons all-purpose flour
4 cups chicken broth
3 slices veggie bacon, cooked, crumbled
1½ pounds baking potatoes (about 4-5), baked, peeled and diced
1 teaspoon salt
½ teaspoon black pepper
1 cup milk
1 cup sour cream
1 cup cheddar cheese
1 tablespoon chives

1. In a medium saucepan, melt butter; add onion, red bell pepper, and garlic. Cook over medium heat until tender, about 5 minutes.

2. In small bowl, combine flour with ¼ cup chicken broth; add to saucepan along with remaining chicken broth, bacon, potatoes, salt, and pepper. Cover; cook over low heat for 25-35 minutes, or until vegetables are soft; stir occasionally.

3. Lightly mash potatoes, leaving some lumps.

4. Add milk, sour cream and cheese; stir until smooth and heated throughout, but not boiling.

5. Sprinkle each serving with chives.

Serves: 6

MINESTRONE

This delicious vegetable soup can also satisfy meat lovers by adding cooked ground sausage, beef, or turkey to it as it simmers.

2 tablespoons olive oil
1 cup onion, finely chopped
1 clove garlic, finely chopped
¾ cup carrots, thinly sliced
5 cups chicken broth
¾ cup green beans
1 tablespoon parsley flakes
1 bay leaf
1 (14-ounce) can tomatoes, diced
1½ cups green cabbage, shredded
1 cup great northern beans, cooked
1 tablespoon dried celery flakes
½ teaspoon salt
¼ teaspoon black pepper
½ cup elbow macaroni, uncooked

1. In a large saucepan, heat oil; add onion, garlic, and carrots; cook over low heat until vegetables begin to soften, about 5 minutes.
2. Add broth; bring to near boiling, reduce heat and add cabbage, beans, celery flakes, salt, and pepper.
3. Cover; cook over low heat for 2 hours, or until vegetables are tender, stirring occasionally.

4. Add uncooked macaroni; cover and continue cooking over low heat for 20 minutes, or until macaroni is tender. Remove bay leaf before serving.

Serves: 6 - 8

SIMPLE MEATBALL SOUP

This is a dish my mother started making years ago as a way to make a fast yet tasty meal. We enjoy the soup with buttery crackers broken into the bowl before eating. A variation I've made is to substitute cooked ground beef for the meatballs and to add more green peppers (for the pepper lover!).

2 teaspoons olive oil
1 small onion, finely chopped
2 cloves garlic, finely chopped
2 cups tomato juice
2 cups beef broth
½ cup water
¾ cup vegetable juice blend (such as V8)
½ cup green pepper, finely chopped
⅓ cup white rice, uncooked
24 meatballs, prepackaged, frozen

1. In a large saucepan, heat olive oil; add onion and garlic, cook over medium heat until onions and garlic are softened, about 5 minutes.
2. Add tomato juice, broth, water, vegetable juice, and green pepper; bring to near boiling then reduce heat. Cover; cook over low heat 30 minutes, or until onions and peppers are soft and flavors are well blended; stir occasionally.
3. Add rice and meatballs; cover and continue cooking for 25 minutes, or until rice is tender and meatballs are heated throughout.
Serves: 4 - 6

SPLIT PEA AND HAM SOUP

This soup can be made thinner or thicker, according to your tastes, by simply adding more water or broth for a thinner soup and using less for a thicker soup.

1 (16-ounce) package dried split peas
2 quarts water
1 (5-ounce) can smoked ground ham, crumbled
2 (14-ounce) cans chicken broth
2½ cups water
1 cup onions, finely chopped
1 cup carrots, shredded
2 cloves garlic, finely chopped
1 tablespoon dried celery flakes
1 teaspoon salt
½ teaspoon black pepper
1 bay leaf

1. Wash peas according to package directions.
2. In a large saucepan, heat 2 quarts water to boiling; remove from heat, add peas. Cover and let sit for one hour to soften peas; drain.
3. Add ham, broth, water, onions, carrots, garlic, celery flakes, salt and pepper. Cover; cook on low heat for 2-3 hours, or until peas are mushy. Stir occasionally.
4. Remove bay leaf; serve.
Serves: 8

TURKEY RICE SOUP

This wonderful broth soup can be turned into a cream-style soup simply by stirring in 1 cup of milk or half-and-half at the end. Either way, it is a satisfying meal in itself, or with rolls, biscuits, or bread on the side.

2 tablespoons olive oil
½ cup onion, finely chopped
2 cloves garlic, finely chopped
2 (14-ounce) cans chicken broth
½ cup water
1 cup turkey, cooked and finely chopped
1 cup green beans
¼ cup red bell peppers, chopped
1 tablespoon celery flakes
1 cup carrots, peeled and thinly sliced or shredded
½ cup white or brown rice, uncooked
½ teaspoon basil
¼ teaspoon black pepper

1. In a medium saucepan, heat oil; add onion and garlic, cook over low heat until softened, about 5 minutes.
2. Add broth, water, turkey, green beans, red pepper, celery flakes, carrots, rice, basil salt and pepper; bring to near boiling then reduce heat.
3. Cover; cook over low heat for 1 hour, or until vegetables are tender.
Serves: 6

VEGETABLE BEEF SOUP

For vegetable lovers, add more vegetables to create an even thicker, heartier soup, and you can leave out the beef altogether for a simple vegetable soup. For meat lovers, you can double the amount of beef to create a heartier soup.

½ pound ground beef
3 cups water
2 (15-ounce) cans beef broth
1 medium onion, finely chopped
1 tablespoon dried celery flakes
1 cup peas
1 cup green beans
1 cup green cabbage, finely chopped
1 cup carrots, thinly sliced
1 medium potato, peeled, diced
1 (16-ounce) can diced tomatoes, undrained
½ teaspoon black pepper
1 teaspoon seasoned salt
¼ teaspoon thyme
1 bay leaf

1. In a large saucepan, cook ground beef, stirring until ground beef is browned and crumbly. Drain fat.
2. Add water, broth, onion, celery, peas, green beans, cabbage, carrots, potato, tomatoes, pepper, seasoned salt, thyme and bay leaf.
3. Cover; cook over low heat for 2 hours, or until vegetables are tender; stir occasionally.
4. Remove bay leaf; serve.
Serves: 6 - 8

ZUCCHINI-POTATO SOUP

Absolutely one of my favorite soups. Light and refreshing, a pure delight. For additional nutrients, and a dash of color, you can add a half cup of cooked shredded carrots after the soup is blended.

1 tablespoon butter
1 cup onion, chopped
4 cups zucchini, peeled and sliced
2 medium potatoes, peeled and diced
1 (14½-ounce) can chicken broth, with roasted garlic and herbs*
1 (14½-ounce) can chicken broth, plain
½ teaspoon white pepper

1. In a large saucepan, melt butter; add onion and cook over low heat until softened, about 5 minutes.

2. Add zucchini, potatoes, broth, and white pepper.

3. Cover; cook over low heat for 45 minutes, or until vegetables are tender.

4. Place half the mixture into a blender; blend until smooth. Pour blended soup into another saucepan or large bowl then blend the remaining half of the vegetables until smooth.

Serves: 4

*If you can't find chicken broth with roasted garlic and herbs, use a can of plain chicken broth and add garlic and your favorite soup herbs. I use a dash of rosemary, thyme, oregano and a little red bell pepper. You may prefer basil, parsley, a bay leaf, etc.

DESSERTS

APPLE COOKIES

Adding just a thin glazing of butter frosting on top of the cooled cookies is all you need to turn these healthy cookies into a sweet treat.

2 cups all-purpose or light baking flour
1 teaspoon baking soda
1/8 teaspoon baking powder
1/2 teaspoon salt
1 teaspoon cinnamon
1/4 teaspoon nutmeg
1/2 cup butter
1 cup brown sugar
1 teaspoon vanilla
1 egg
1/4 cup milk
1 heaping tablespoon applesauce
1 cup apples, peeled and shredded or grated
1/2 cup raisins, plumper & moister style (optional)
frosting (page 252)

Heat oven to 375 degrees

1. In a medium bowl, combine flour, baking soda, baking powder, salt, cinnamon and nutmeg; set aside.
2. In a large bowl, cream butter, sugar and vanilla; add egg and mix well, stir in milk and applesauce.
3. Add flour mixture, stirring just until the dry ingredients are moistened and a few lumps remain; fold in apples, and raisins if desired.

4. Drop by teaspoonfuls onto greased baking sheet; bake for 10-12 minutes.

5. Cool, and lightly frost.

Yield: 3 dozen

Applesauce Cookies

These cookies are moist and cake-like. My niece calls them "muffin-like cookies", and prefers them without the frosting.

2 cups all-purpose or light baking flour
1 teaspoon baking soda
¼ teaspoon salt
1 teaspoon cinnamon
1 teaspoon ginger
¼ teaspoon cloves
½ cup butter, softened
½ cup brown sugar
¼ cup white sugar
1 egg
1 cup applesauce
1 cup raisins, moister & plumper style (optional)
frosting (page 252)

Heat oven to 350 degrees

1. In a medium bowl, combine flour, baking soda, salt, cinnamon, ginger and cloves; set aside.
2. In a large bowl, beat butter, brown sugar and white sugar together; add egg and beat until smooth.
3. Stir in applesauce, then gradually stir in flour mixture; mixing just until the dry ingredients are moistened and a few lumps remain; fold in raisins if desired.

4. Drop by tablespoonfuls onto greased baking sheet about 2 inches apart. Bake in a 350 degree oven for 8-10 minutes, or until lightly browned.

5. Cool; lightly frost.

Yield: 2 dozen

BAKED EGG CUSTARD

The smooth, silky texture, and the light luscious taste, is pure heaven. Try it, you'll like it!

3 eggs, lightly beaten
2 cups milk
½ cup granulated sugar
½ teaspoon vanilla
¼ teaspoon salt
½ teaspoon cinnamon or nutmeg (optional)

Heat oven to 350 degrees

1. In a large bowl, beat eggs; add milk, sugar, vanilla, and salt; beat or whisk until well blended.
2. Pour into greased 1½ -quart baking dish; sprinkle with cinnamon or nutmeg if desired.
3. Set baking dish in a pan of shallow water; bake in a 350 degree oven for 40 minutes, or until knife inserted in center comes out clean.
Serves: 6

Banana Marshmallow Gelatin

If you love marshmallows, this is the dessert for you. Light and fluffy, you can try this with a variety of fresh, soft fruit.

1 (.3-ounce) package flavored gelatin
1 cup boiling water
1 cup cold water
2 medium bananas, peeled and sliced
1 cup miniature marshmallows

1. In a medium bowl, dissolve gelatin in hot water, stirring constantly.
2. When gelatin is dissolved, add cold water and stir to blend; refrigerate to chill.
3. When almost set, gently fold in banana slices and marshmallows; refrigerate until firm.
Serves: 6

CARROT CAKE

A lovely, light dessert that is oh – so good for you, too. This dessert has crushed pineapple, which may not be soft enough for everyone.

2 cups all-purpose or light baking flour
2 teaspoons baking soda
¼ teaspoon baking powder
2 teaspoons cinnamon
1 cup brown sugar
2 large eggs
⅔ cup buttermilk
1 (8-ounce) can crushed pineapple, undrained
3 tablespoons vegetable oil
1 teaspoon vanilla
2 cups carrots, shredded
 whipped cream or frosting (page 252)

Heat oven to 350 degrees

1. In a medium bowl, combine flour, baking soda, baking powder, and cinnamon; set aside.
2. In a large bowl, beat together sugar and eggs; add buttermilk, pineapple with juice, oil, and vanilla, beating until well combined.
3. Gradually add flour mixture, beating until batter is smooth; fold in carrots.
4. Pour into a greased 13x9-inch baking dish; bake in a 350 degree oven for 30 minutes, or until toothpick inserted in center comes out clean.
5. Cool; top each serving with whipped cream or frosting.
Serves: 12 - 15

Chocolate Buttermilk Cake

This chocolate cake with chocolate cream cheese frosting is a chocolate lovers dream. Besides being doubly chocolate delicious, it is light and fluffy. Be sure to use an electric mixer as that helps ensure lightness to cake and frosting alike.

¼ cup cocoa, sifted
1½ cups light baking flour or cake flour
¾ teaspoon baking soda
½ teaspoon salt
½ cup butter
¾ cup sugar
½ teaspoon vanilla
1 egg
1 cup buttermilk

Chocolate Cream Cheese Frosting
1½ ounces unsweetened chocolate
3 ounces cream cheese, softened
¼ cup butter
1½ -2 cups powdered sugar
1 tablespoon milk

Heat oven to 350 degrees

1. In a medium bowl, combine cocoa, flour, baking soda, and salt; set aside.

2. In a large bowl, beat butter and sugar together until smooth; beat in egg then vanilla.

3. Add flour mixture to butter mixture alternately with buttermilk, beating just until smooth and well blended.

4. Pour batter into greased 9x9-inch baking dish. Bake in a 350 degree oven for 30 minutes, or until toothpick inserted in center comes out clean; set aside to cool.

5. Meanwhile, in a medium bowl, melt chocolate in microwave; add soft cream cheese and soft butter and beat until fluffy.

6. Slowly add powdered sugar along with milk; continue beating until fluffy.

7. Frost cooled cake; serve.

Serves: 9

CREAMY STRAWBERRY GELATIN

A cool and light dessert, perfect on a summer day or anytime.

1 (.3-ounce) package strawberry flavored gelatin
1 cup hot water
¾ cup cold water
1 (8-ounce) container strawberry yogurt

1. In a medium bowl, dissolve gelatin in hot water, stirring constantly.

2. When gelatin is dissolved, add cold water and stir to blend; refrigerate to chill.

3. When slightly thickened, add yogurt and beat with an electric mixer until mixture is light and fluffy.

4. Pour into individual serving dishes; refrigerate to chill until firm.

Serves: 6

CUSTARD PIE

This is a traditional recipe of this smooth, mild tasting dessert. If you crave more flavor, try adding lemon or orange peel into the mixture or add some cinnamon with the nutmeg on top.

⅓ cup sugar
2 teaspoons flour
½ teaspoon salt
3 eggs
3 cups milk or half-and-half
¼ teaspoon nutmeg
1 (9-inch) pie shell, unbaked

Heat oven to 350 degrees

1. In a medium bowl, beat sugar, flour, salt and eggs.
2. Add 1 cup of milk to egg mixture; beat or whisk until smooth. Add remaining milk.
3. Place empty pie shell on baking sheet; pour egg mixture into pie shell and sprinkle nutmeg on top.
4. Bake in a 350 degree oven for 45 minutes, or until center is set.
Serves: 8

EASY DEEP-DISH APPLE PIE

So deceptively simple to make, so incredibly delicious to eat. You could also add a peeled and chopped fresh pear along with the apples for an interesting variation. Pile the fruit high, and enjoy the result.

2 pre-made frozen or refrigerated pie crusts
6–8 cooking apples
½ cup sugar
1 tablespoon all-purpose flour
1 teaspoon cinnamon
1 teaspoon butter

Heat oven to 350 degrees

1. Peel and core apples; cut into slices and place in a large bowl.
2. In a small bowl, combine sugar, flour and cinnamon; sprinkle evenly over apples, tossing to combine.
3. Place one pie crust into a pie plate (unless it comes in its own pan); transfer apple slices into the pie crust, piling them several inches higher than the crust rim.
4. Break butter into small pieces and dot across top.
5. Lay remaining pie crust over pie, pinch edges to seal.
6. Cut a ½-inch hole in the top center to let steam escape; place on a baking sheet to catch any juices that overflow and bake in a 350 degree oven for 50 minutes, or until apples are tender and the top crust is browned.
Serves: 8

HOT PEACHES AND DUMPLINGS

Fresh summer peaches cooked until the juices flow, topped with homemade sweet dumplings. Add a scoop of vanilla ice cream and taste the goodness of summer.

2 cups fresh peaches, sliced
⅛ cup maple syrup
⅛ cup water
½ teaspoon cinnamon
⅛ teaspoon allspice or nutmeg

Dumplings
1 tablespoon butter, melted
½ cup all-purpose or light baking flour
1 teaspoon baking powder
¼ teaspoon salt
2 tablespoons granulated sugar
¼ cup milk
cinnamon sugar

1. In a medium saucepan, add peaches, maple syrup, water, cinnamon, and allspice or nutmeg; cover, cook over low heat until peaches are at boiling stage, about 10 minutes.

2. Meanwhile, in a medium bowl, combine butter, flour, baking powder, salt sugar, and milk; mix just until smooth.

3. Drop spoonfuls of flour mixture onto the hot peach mixture; cover and cook on medium heat for 10-12 minutes, or until dumplings are cooked throughout.

4. Sprinkle dumplings with cinnamon sugar and serve.

Serves: 4

PUMPKIN BARS

These "cookie" bars are incredibly soft and moist. Once, when I didn't have a jelly roll pan on hand, I just spooned the dough into mini-muffin tins. They turned out beautifully and each one was a perfect bite-size.

2 cups all-purpose or light baking flour
2 teaspoons baking powder
1 teaspoon baking soda
2 teaspoons pumpkin pie spice
1 teaspoon salt
4 eggs, lightly beaten
1½ cups sugar
1 cup vegetable oil
1 (15-ounce) can pumpkin puree
frosting (page 252)

Heat oven to 350 degrees

1. In a medium bowl, combine flour, baking powder, baking soda, pumpkin pie spice and salt; set aside.
2. In a medium bowl, add eggs, sugar, oil, and pumpkin; mix with an electric beater until fluffy.
3. Slowly add flour mixture to egg mixture, mixing just until the dry ingredients are moistened and a few lumps remain.
4. Spread batter evenly into ungreased 11x15-inch baking dish or jellyroll pan. Bake at 350 degrees for 25 minutes, or until lightly browned and toothpick inserted in center comes out clean.
5. Allow to cool; spread with frosting and cut into squares.
Yield: 24

PUMPKIN BUNDT CAKE

For Thanksgiving, or anytime, this moist, delicious cake is sure to please.

3 cups all-purpose or light baking flour
2 teaspoons baking powder
2 teaspoons baking soda
½ teaspoon salt
2 teaspoons pumpkin pie spice
4 eggs
1½ cups sugar
¾ cup vegetable oil
2 cups canned pumpkin
¼ cup applesauce
½ cup walnuts, finely ground (optional)
powdered sugar or icing (page 253)

Heat oven to 350 degrees

1. In a medium bowl, combine flour, baking powder, baking soda, salt and pumpkin pie spice; set aside.
2. In a large bowl, beat eggs and sugar together; beat in oil, pumpkin, and applesauce.
3. Add dry ingredients, and ground walnuts if desired; continue beating just until smooth and well blended.
4. Pour into a greased Bundt pan; bake in a 350 degree oven for 1 hour and 15 minutes, or until a toothpick inserted in center comes out clean.

5. Cool; turn pan upside down over a cake plate to remove cake. Dust top with powdered sugar or drizzle with icing.

Serves: 12 - 15

RHUBARB CAKE

Rhubarb is surprisingly easy to peel. Just wash the stalks, cut off the dried ends, then peel off the outer layer of stringy stalk. The rhubarb makes this cake moist and light.

2 cups all-purpose or light baking flour
1 teaspoon cinnamon
1 teaspoon baking soda
½ teaspoon salt
½ cup butter, softened
1 cup sugar
1 egg
1 teaspoon vanilla
1 cup buttermilk
2 cups rhubarb, finely chopped
½ cup walnuts, finely ground (optional)
frosting (page 252) or whipped cream

Heat oven to 350 degrees

1. In a medium bowl, combine flour, cinnamon, baking soda and salt; set aside.
2. In a large bowl, beat butter and sugar together; add egg and vanilla, continue beating until smooth.
3. Alternately add buttermilk and flour mixture until well blended; fold in rhubarb, plus walnuts if desired.
4. Pour into a greased 9x13-inch baking dish; bake at 350 degrees for 30 minutes, or until toothpick inserted in center comes out clean.
5. Frost, or top each serving with whipped cream.
Serves: 12 – 15

SOFT CHOCOLATE COOKIES

The pureed cottage cheese in this recipe makes these cookies moist plus gives this dessert an extra protein punch.

1 cup butter, softened
¾ cup granulated sugar
½ cup brown sugar
2 teaspoons vanilla
2 eggs, lightly beaten
1 cup cottage cheese, pureed
½ cup cocoa powder, sifted
2¾ cup all-purpose or light baking flour
1 teaspoon baking powder
½ teaspoon baking soda
powdered sugar

Heat oven to 350 degrees

1. In a medium bowl, cream together butter and sugars; add vanilla, eggs, and cottage cheese; beat until smooth.
2. Add cocoa powder, flour, baking powder and baking soda; beat just until blended. Cover; place in refrigerator to chill, approximately 2 hours.
3. Using heaping tablespoonfuls roll dough into balls; roll each ball in powdered sugar and place on greased baking sheet.
4. Bake in a 350 degree oven for 12 minutes.
Yield: 5 dozen

SUPERB PUMPKIN PIE

Yes, this pie is rich, but the real cream in the recipe is what makes it so, well—creamy. It is smooth, delicious and easy to get down!

1(15-ounce) can pumpkin
¾ cup light brown sugar
1½ teaspoons ginger
¾ teaspoon cinnamon
¼ teaspoon nutmeg
¼ teaspoon salt
3 large eggs, beaten
1¼ cups heavy whipping cream
1 9-inch deep dish pie crust

Heat oven to 350 degrees

1. In a small saucepan, combine pumpkin, sugar, ginger, cinnamon, nutmeg and salt; cook over medium heat for 5 minutes, stirring frequently.
2. Transfer pumpkin mixture to a blender; blend for 10 seconds, then add eggs, one at a time, pulsing blender between each addition.
3. Slowly add cream to blender, blend just until well mixed.
4. Pour pumpkin pie mixture into pie crust; bake in a 350 degree oven for 1 hour, or until center is set and knife inserted into center comes out clean.
Serves: 8

Sweet Potato Chocolate Chip Cookies

Think you can't eat chocolate chips? The chocolate chips are melt-in-your-mouth soft while still warm from the oven. To eat after they have cooled, simply heat in the microwave oven for a few seconds to soften the chips. This cookie will be softer yet if you leave out the chips, then frost.

1¾ cups all-purpose or light baking flour
1 teaspoon baking soda
1 teaspoon baking powder
¼ teaspoon salt
¾ teaspoon cinnamon
¾ cup sweet potatoes, cooked and mashed
½ cup butter, softened
¼ cup cream cheese, softened
⅓ cup applesauce
2 eggs, lightly beaten
½ cup brown sugar
½ cup granulated sugar
1 teaspoon vanilla
1 cup semisweet chocolate chips

Heat oven to 350 degrees

1. In a medium bowl, combine flour, baking soda, baking powder, salt, and cinnamon; set aside.

2. In a large bowl, using an electric mixer, beat sweet potatoes, butter, cream cheese, applesauce, eggs, sugars and vanilla together, beating just until smooth.

3. Gradually beat flour mixture into sweet potato mixture; fold in chocolate chips.

4. Drop by tablespoonfuls onto ungreased baking sheets; bake in a 350 degree oven for 12-15 minutes, or until lightly browned.

Yield: 2 dozen

TAPIOCA PUDDING

This has always been my mother's favorite pudding, so it's been made often at our house.

4 cups milk
⅓ cup tapioca
3 eggs
1 cup sugar
1 teaspoon vanilla
whipped cream (optional)

1. In a medium saucepan, heat milk until near boiling; reduce heat and add tapioca, cook on low heat for 20 minutes, or until tapioca is translucent. Stir occasionally.

2. In a small bowl, beat eggs, sugar and vanilla together; slowly add egg mixture to saucepan; continue cooking over low heat and stirring constantly until pudding thickens to desired consistency.

3. Refrigerate to chill. Top each serving with whipped cream if desired.

Serves: 6

TENDER SUGAR COOKIES

The buttermilk in this sugar cookie recipe adds moisture and tenderness.

2 cups all-purpose or light baking flour
¼ teaspoon salt
¾ teaspoon baking soda
1 teaspoon cinnamon
¼ cup butter, softened
1 cup sugar
1 egg, lightly beaten
½ cup buttermilk
frosting (page 252)

Heat oven to 350 degrees

1. In a medium bowl, combine flour, salt, baking soda and cinnamon; set aside.
2. In a large bowl, beat butter and sugar together until fluffy; add egg and milk; continue beating until smooth.
3. Stir flour mixture into egg mixture, stirring just until well blended.
4. Drop by tablespoonfuls onto a greased baking sheet, about 2-inches apart.
5. Bake in a 350 degree oven for 10 minutes, or until lightly browned.
6. Lightly spread cooled cookies with frosting.
Yield: 2 dozen

TOMATO JUICE CAKE

The result is a very moist cake, and no – it does not taste like tomatoes! It won't rise as high as most cakes, so just cut it into bars to serve and eat it like a Texas Sheet Cake or bar cookie.

1¼ cups all-purpose or light baking flour
½ teaspoon baking soda
2 teaspoons baking powder
½ teaspoon salt
1 teaspoon cinnamon
¼ teaspoon cloves
¼ teaspoon nutmeg
½ teaspoon allspice
⅓ cup butter, softened
¼ cup applesauce
¾ cup sugar
2 large eggs
1 cup tomato juice
½ cup golden raisins (optional)
½ cups walnuts, finely ground (optional)
cream cheese frosting (page 252)

Heat oven to 350 degrees

1. In a medium bowl, combine flour, baking soda, baking powder, salt and spices; set aside.
2. In a large bowl, beat butter, applesauce and sugar together until fluffy; beat in eggs one at a time.

247

3. Add flour mixture alternately with tomato juice, beating just until blended; fold in raisins and ground walnuts if desired.

4. Pour batter into greased 13x9-inch baking dish; bake in a 350 degree oven for 25 minutes, or until toothpick inserted in center comes out clean. Cool; frost.

Serves: 12 – 15

WALNUT CAKE

Surprisingly light and tender. You don't have to give up the flavor of nuts just because you need soft food.

3½ cups all-purpose or light baking flour
2 teaspoons baking soda
¼ teaspoon baking powder
½ teaspoon salt
½ cup butter, softened
½ cup vegetable oil
1 cup sugar
4 large eggs
1½ cups buttermilk
1 teaspoon vanilla
1½ cups walnuts, finely ground
frosting (page 252)

Heat oven to 350 degrees

1. In a medium bowl, combine flour, baking soda, baking powder, and salt; set aside.
2. In a large bowl, beat butter, oil and sugar together until smooth; beat in eggs one at a time, then vanilla.
3. Add flour mixture to egg mixture alternately with buttermilk, beating just until smooth and blended fold in ground walnuts.
4. Pour batter into greased 13x9-inch baking dish; bake at 350 degrees for 35 minutes, or until toothpick inserted in center comes out clean. Cool; frost.

Serves: 12 - 15

YOGURT SPICE BUNDT CAKE

Delicious. The yogurt makes it moist, the spice gives it just the right flavor. Be sure to use your electric mixer – it helps this cake turn out so light!

2 cups all-purpose or light baking flour
1 teaspoon cinnamon
1 teaspoon allspice
½ teaspoon nutmeg
½ teaspoon salt
1½ teaspoons baking soda
1¼ cups sugar
1 cup butter, softened
3 eggs
1 cup plain or vanilla yogurt
1 teaspoon vanilla
powdered sugar or frosting (page 252)

Heat oven to 325 degrees

1. In a medium bowl, combine flour, cinnamon, allspice, nutmeg, salt, and baking soda; set aside.
2. In a large bowl, beat sugar and butter together.
3. Add eggs one at a time; add yogurt, vanilla, and flour mixture, beating just until blended
4. Pour batter into a greased Bundt pan; bake in a 325 degree oven for 45 minutes, or until a toothpick inserted in center comes out clean.
5. Cool; turn pan upside down over a cake plate to remove cake. Dust top with powdered sugar or frost.
Serves: 12 – 15

ZUCCHINI COOKIES

The lemon in these tender cookies adds that "special something" to the taste, letting them taste as light as they feel.

½ cup butter, softened
¼ cup applesauce
¾ cup sugar
1 egg, lightly beaten
1 teaspoon lemon peel powder
2 cups all-purpose or light baking flour
1¼ teaspoon baking powder
½ teaspoon salt
1½ cup zucchini, peeled and shredded
½ cup walnuts or pecans, finely ground (optional)
frosting (page 252)

Heat oven to 350 degrees

1. In a medium bowl, beat together butter, applesauce and sugar until fluffy; add egg and continue beating.
2. Stir in lemon peel powder, flour, baking powder and salt; mix just until well blended.
3. Fold in zucchini, and nuts if desired.
4. Place on greased baking sheet by tablespoonfuls; bake in a 350 degree oven for 15 minutes.
5. Cool; frost.
Yield: 1½ dozen

FROSTINGS

BUTTER CREAM FROSTING
This will frost a two layer cake or a 13x9x2-inch cake.

½ cup butter, softened
4 cups powdered sugar
1 teaspoon vanilla
3 tablespoons milk

1. In a large bowl, using an electric mixer, combine all ingredients until creamy.
2. Add more milk, one teaspoon at a time, if needed for easy spreading.

CREAM CHEESE FROSTING
This will frost a two layer cake or a 13x9x2-inch cake.

1 (3-ounce) package cream cheese, softened
¼ cup butter, softened
1 teaspoon vanilla
3 cups powdered sugar

1. In a large bowl, using an electric mixer, beat cream cheese, butter, and vanilla until light and fluffy.
2. Gradually add powdered sugar, mixing well. Add more powdered sugar, or a teaspoon of milk, if needed for easy spreading.

Icing

This is a light glazing for cookies or to drizzle over a dessert.

½ cup powdered sugar
¼ teaspoon vanilla
3 teaspoons milk

1. In a small bowl, combine all ingredients until well blended and smooth.

INDEX

ABOUT THE AUTHOR

Kristine Benishek is a medical librarian with over twenty years experience as a manager of medical libraries in academic hospitals. She is a member of the Ohio Health Sciences Library Association, the Medical Library Association, and the Academy of Health Information Professionals. Throughout her career she has worked closely with healthcare professionals in meeting their informational needs related to patient care and assessing quality of life issues. For several years she wrote reviews of forthcoming health care books for the *Library Journal* and also served on her county's Public Health Department Healthy People 2010 committee.

Printed in Great Britain
by Amazon